HOW T
FAMOUS
RESTAURANT
RECIPES

50 Favorite Copycat Famous Restaurant Dishes You Can Easily Make at Home

By

Isabella Collins

Copyright © Autumn Leaf Publishing Press, 2020

Email: Publisher@AutumnLeafPub@gmail.com

All Rights Reserved.

Without limiting the rights under the copyright laws, no part of this publication may be reproduced, stored in or introduced into a retrieval system, or transmitted, in any form or by any means (electronic, mechanical, photocopying, recording or otherwise), without the prior written consent of the publisher of this book.

Autumn Leaf Publishing Press publishes its books and guides in a variety of electronic and print formats, Some content that appears in print may not be available in electronic format, and vice versa.

Design & Illustration by Jordy Roberts

First Edition

Contents

Introduction 7

Home cooked Benefits 15

    It's Therapeutic 15

    It's Results-Oriented 17

    It's Enhancing 18

    It's a Social Activity 20

    It's Cheaper 21

    It's Nourishing 22

    It Enables You to Have Control 24

    It's Unifying 25

Breakfast Recipes 27

    IHOP's Bacon Temptation Omelet 31

    El Papi's Avocado Tomatillo Tacos 33

    Denny's Pancake Puppies 36

    The Grand Lux Café's Chicken-N-Waffles 38

    IHOP's Banana Pancakes 43

    McDonald's Egg White Delight 47

    Danny's Donuts French Toast 49

    McDonald's Ham and Egg Sandwiches 51

Fast Food Alternative Overnight Oats 54

Dunkin Donuts Chocolate Chip Muffins..........................57

Appetizer Recipes 61

Texas Roadhouse Rolls and Cinnamon Butter.................63

Fat Ronnie's Deep-Fried Mushrooms 67

Olive Garden Spinach Artichoke Dip 70

Applebee's Veggie Patch Pizza 73

Wingstop Garlic Parmesan Wings 76

Hooters Hot Wings...80

Olive Garden Lasagna Dip and Pasta Chips.....................82

Cheddars Scratch Kitchen Cheese Fries 85

Lunch Recipes 87

Wendy's Grilled Chicken Sandwich...................................89

Chipotle Burrito Bowls 92

Alonti's Pecan Pesto Pasta 96

Olive Garden Steak Gorgonzola Alfredo...........................97

Chick fil A Mac and Cheese 101

Red Lobster Lobster Pizza 103

Bucca di Beppo's Three Meat Sauce 106

Dinner Recipes 108

Panda Express Beijing Beef...110

San Jacinto Pork Carnitas 113

Romano's Macaroni Grill Chicken Rigatoni 116

Olive Garden Zuppa Toscana 119

Cajun Café Bourbon Chicken... 121

Jay's Oyster House Baked Parmesan Shrimp.................... 123

Side Dishes.. 125

Cracker Barrel Sprouts and Kale Salad............................. 126

KFC Coleslaw... 129

KFC Potato Wedges 131

Lee's Famous Recipe Corn on the Cob............................. 134

Dickey's Barbecue Baked Potato Casserole 136

Boston Market Creamed Spinach 138

Wendy's Fondue Fries.. 140

Dessert Recipes... 142

Taco Bell Cinnamon Twists.. 143

Shoney's Hot Fudge Cake... 144

Cracker Barrel Coke Cake 148

Reese's Peanut Butter Eggs 151

Applebee's Blond Brownies.. 153

Zapato's Barbecue Banana Pudding 156

Drink Recipes.. 159

McDonald's Thin Mint Milkshake 160

Red Robin Screaming Red Zombie 161

Starbucks Hibiscus Refresher 163

Dunkin Donuts Caramel Hot Chocolate 165

Taco Bell Baja Blast Freeze..167

Chili's Green Apple Sangria 168

Copycat Cooking and Health 170

Healthy Substitutes...171

Allergen-friendly Foods..173

Conclusion 184

Introduction

According to George Bernard Shaw, "There is no sincerer love than the love of food."

Well, as a strong foodie, I totally agree with this. I do not know about you, but my taste buds have always been much enhanced in their skills, unlike my skills in the kitchen with pots and pans.

It is expected in most countries that a lady must be good in the kitchen and should not have a problem finding her way around the kitchen. While there is a constant shift in society and a lot of men all over the world are embracing kitchen work, it is generally the role of the woman to cook for her family. Our mother was very keen on reminding us of that every single day.

So, with that in mind, I developed an interest in cooking and begun learning how to make different cuisines and master the different flavorings. My mother was a very good cook. I still remember some of her dishes and cook them once in a while. She taught me quite a lot and inspired me to cook better and healthier foods.

I grew up in Arizona around great people who were deep-rooted in their culture. We enjoyed nature, a lot of cultural activities, and the older people were keen on teaching us culture and gender roles as culture has it. My life, however, took quite a turn after I finished high school. My mother passed away following a long fight with cancer. My father had always been a hardworking man. He did a lot of jobs so as to put food on the table for us.

Things were very difficult when mom fell sick since the medical bills would take up most of the income that my parents earned. As the firstborn in our family, it was difficult watching my parents suffer. It was difficult watching my mother struggle to accomplish activities that she previously found very easy to do. The least I could do was to help around the house anytime I came home from school.

After mom's death, it became more difficult for my father as there were things that he could not do as well as my mom. He had other greater priorities to undertake that he needed help around the house. As the eldest child in a family of five siblings, it automatically became my role to take care of my siblings. This included cleaning, doing shopping, and, most definitely, cooking.

Due to my father's low income, I also had to take up a number of service jobs to support my father in taking care of my siblings, who were still in school. Most of these jobs were in hotels, where I sometimes did cleaning in the kitchen or worked as a sous chef. With the little knowledge I had on kitchen stuff, I did not find it very hard to work around the kitchen. Thanks to my mom. I appreciated some jobs I was given as I would use some awesome kitchen tricks that my mom taught me. I thank God I also had good bosses who were very understanding and willing to teach me a lot.

I would apply those skills at home with my siblings. I would practice at home, cooking every dish I would watch being cooked in the kitchen. My siblings really loved this because they would have delicious meals constantly, including some that they had never tasted before. They really enjoyed the experiments. They still ask me to cook some of those dishes when we have a family get-together at our places. Sometimes my brother comes over with ingredients of his favorite chicken dish and asks me to prepare it for him.

Eventually, I went to college and then got married to a very good man. My husband is also a foodie and enjoys eating different kinds of delicacies. For this reason, I have tried quite a number of new dishes in my small kitchen. My family is very supportive and helps a lot in these food adventures. When at home, I am always running around the kitchen and always busy creating different kinds of dishes from all over the world. Along with taking care of my husband and kids, I can barely get the time to relax and have time to myself. However, I will never tire or complain as it is something that I enjoy very much and always look forward to.

We frequently entertain guests. I like watching them savor the dishes I make. It encourages me to look for more recipes and make them. I always feel like it is up to me to ensure that my family enjoys the best of dishes. It is my responsibility to ensure my family and friends get the best quality of food when at my place.

Even though I make good food, we enjoy going to restaurants once in a while. It is always a good experience going out and getting a feel of other peoples' prowess in the kitchen. My husband loves Outback Steakhouse, who offers some of the best steaks in the country. We go there a lot, including some other restaurants like BJ's Restaurant and Brew House, which offers the best deep-dish pizzas I have ever tasted.

Doing rounds around the restaurant circuit is always a great experience as each time has its own epic food encounter. I always try my best to eat a different dish from the previous one when I get to go back to a hotel I have visited before. I also try out restaurants that belong to other people from other countries. This is always great because I get to taste different foods made from other places besides the U.S. This has allowed me to taste a vast array of cuisines from different parts of the world such as China, India, Ethiopia, and even Kenya. Tasting different foods has helped me understand and appreciate different cultures in the world.

It always feels good to experience new cultures, and there is no better way of experiencing it than through food.

Due to the several jobs in restaurants, I have been lucky enough to have good friends who are not only foodies but good cooks as well. Some are even better in the kitchen than I am. My best friend, Lucy, makes the best chicken wings ever. She is talented in making some very sweet and juicy chicken wings that even my kids admit are better than mine. She once taught me her recipe, but I could swear she has a secret ingredient that she did not tell me about. No matter what I do, my chicken wings are never as good as hers.

However, I enjoy spending time cooking with her and later enjoying the results of our toil.

I have a collection of cookbooks at home that I have used many times over the years. My friends know my love for food and how much I enjoy cooking. For this reason, they usually get me cookbooks every year. My best friend once told me that whenever she sees an interesting cookbook, she thinks of me because she knows how much I would enjoy making the dishes in it. I had to remind them that I have a love for other things besides food, and I would still appreciate other gifts besides cookbooks. (I hope they will remember that this year.) Either way, however, I always appreciate their gifts and love trying out the new things they bring me each year.

Over the years, I have also been blessed enough to become a freelance chef consultant and offer my services to other people who love food as I do. My husband, kids, and friends encouraged me to offer my skills to other people. Realizing my talent and prowess in the kitchen, they urged me to share it with the rest of the world and also earn from it.

With their support, I got my first client in 2013, and that endeavor has grown over the years. With a number of skills up my sleeve, I am able to see to it that my customers receive the best services they could ever get. Though it has not been an easy journey, I must admit that the job was the best business decision I ever made, thanks to my family and friends.

From my job, I got to learn that I had to spend a lot of money at first before I could earn any money. I had to read a lot of success stories from other entrepreneurs so as to be encouraged. It was shocking to find out how some of them spent their nights in the streets, struggling to find shelter from the cold while others had to toil for long-drawn times with little returns. However, they worked hard and persisted through it all until they succeeded.

This really encouraged me to never give up and also seek to offer the best to my customers. I got ideas for my job, which I implemented and have brought great results. One of these ideas is having free offers at certain times throughout the year, which the customers really like. Besides the service they would ask for, I would also give them free advanced recipes on steaks, chicken wings, salads, etc. These ideas were great as they have helped pull in a lot of customers over the years. I always purpose to offer the best services and ensure that my customers are happy and satisfied.

My husband has been very supportive in my consulting business and has taught me a lot about business and dealing with my customers. I, honestly, could not do it without him. He has stood with me every step of the way and ensured that

I overcome every obstacle that has come my way ever since I set up shop. It is not easy for a woman with a family to run her own business. It would be impossible to make any progress without the support of your husband. For this reason, I am very grateful for what he has done for me and for being there for me.

It is my joy, beyond the financial benefit, to see my customers satisfied. No words can express the joy I feel when a client calls me and tells me how much they enjoyed a recipe I gave them, or a restaurant owner tells me his or her customers love some dish I introduced. It is my joy when I see them smile and enjoy the recipes I have taught them. I feel so happy when families and friends come over and bond in events over food I have helped cook. It fills me with so much joy.

I also love reading the comments left by my customers, which really encourages me to push on and become better. Through engaging with my customers, I have learned a lot and made many improvements to my business. I hope to grow and eventually have a restaurant of my own. Through food and interacting with customers, I have come to win the hearts of many, and I hope that number will increase as time goes by.

Home cooked Benefits

So, why cook at home? What exactly is so good about cooking at home?

Well, besides making your family happy, there are very many benefits to cooking at home. For instance, current developments in science currently have it that there are emotional benefits when one cooks. Yes. Science has it that after a long bad day, it might be better to try out stuff in a recipe book rather than automatically collapsing on the couch.

It's Therapeutic

There is a myriad of reasons why you should use cooking as a therapy tool for bad times. There have been cases around the world of people with mood disorders who have received help from programs that use cooking as a technique for therapy. They call it "therapeutic cooking" and have been very vocal in sharing their experiences in the therapy. Many have spoken of its benefits and encouraged people to try it even in their homes. So, this is something that you can copy in your own home. All you need is a few ingredients, a bit of effort, and you are good to go.

Nicole Lambert, a counselor at Movement Counseling Services, says that cooking is very helpful for mental health in that it offers a creative outlet to an individual. With cooking, people get to channel their energy, which would otherwise be used as a distraction. It also assists in building one's prowess in a skill, as well as express his or her emotions through a beneficial medium.

As might be expected, cooking, like exercise, is not easy to accomplish as much as it is very beneficial to one's mental health.

Some cases of mood disorders, like depression, may be different. These cases may lower your appetite and levels of energy, making it very challenging to psyche yourself up to make a dish. However, researchers have revealed that once someone is done cooking, he or she enjoys a lot of mental calmness, even if the outcome is not so complex. These benefits are especially heightened if you are making a meal for more people than just yourself.

If you are considering trying out cooking as a therapy, but are confused about how to begin, do not worry. Do not assume that you will have distinguished skills in the kitchen after your initial attempt. Cooking skill takes practice. All professional chefs and expert home cooks will admit to the fact that it has taken them years for them to perfect their skills and become pros. For starters, you could start small by getting a cookbook for beginners and trying out the recipes. Before you know it, your friends could be calling you for help in the kitchen when they are hosting parties.

It's Results-Oriented

Cooking also helps an individual because it usually yields results. It occupies your mind in activity and later yields results after a while. Activity and results are some of the things that help in mental health.

Cooking results help in mental health because, unlike most results, they are fast and tangible. With them, the individual gets quick and substantial things for their efforts. Cooking results are normally good, with tasty food that the participant consumes. This brings about a good feeling and helps an individual have confidence in the fact that their actions can yield good results.

It also brings about a good feeling. Trying out easy recipes is particularly better because the process does not bring about anxiety to the cook. This, therefore, is very beneficial for strong mental health. Studies show that cooking develops creativity, focus, and happiness. The study was done on a number of people whose actions and movements were monitored closely.

These people often did activities like cooking that were meaningful and calming but small. Due to doing these activities daily, they were observed to be happier than other people around them. These people had confidence in themselves and felt capable of achieving their goals. This is because of accomplishing the activities as well as the creativity that the people applied while cooking. This showed that, indeed, creativity does develop one's life and makes one more confident in themselves.

It's Enhancing

Cooking is essential in our lives and nourishes our lives in many ways. We practice self-care every time we cook. Like alchemy, a cook usually takes ingredients and transmutes them into a delicacy that nourishes the body and soul. It helps us get in touch with who we physically are. When we cook, we allow the things we see and touch in the outer world to communicate with our physical bodies, which are our inner world.

Science backs this up through a study that was done in 2018, where people doing cooking therapy were observed. A number of communities where people do a lot of home cooking were also observed. This study revealed some fascinating outcomes. It was observed that therapeutic cooking brought about some positive impacts on self-esteem, social life, as well as one's quality of life.

It was helpful for the participants to be around others in the cooking classes and programs as it promoted a comfortable feeling within them and also made them feel more confident in themselves. Cooking made them become better in character and overall social life with time.

If you usually feel calmer as you cook, do not be surprised. A lot of people tend to feel calm when cooking. It just gets you in another world. Like meditation, a lot of people have been known to get "in the zone" when cooking. This causes one to lose track of time and put their focus on the task that they are dealing with. This is a very important and helpful thing for people. For those people battling negative thoughts and dealing with fear, doubt, and confusion on a constant basis, cooking can be a good option for relieving the stress they are struggling with. It is a healthy vent that will bring calmness and serenity into your minds.

This later reflects on your physical body. When your mind is at ease, so is your physical body as it responds to the state of mind. You will experience a sort of relaxing feeling. Once you get in the flow of the cooking activity, the tensions that can start rising in our bodies due to anxiety and depression are usually eased.

It's a Social Activity

This even becomes better when you cook for other people. This helps us even more mentally than when we cook for ourselves only. Over the years, people have observed cultural practices that involved cooking for each other and eating together. People would normally gather for the breaking of bread and bonding. Sometimes, cooking has also been used as a gesture to show someone that you care about him or her. This could be done in the occurrence of a crisis, during a celebration, for entertainment, or just nourishment. Those kitchen moments when people bond while cooking is usually very beneficial to an individual.

In Africa, for instance, when a woman gives birth, women in some communities usually cook a lot of black beans and porridge for her. They normally cook them at their homes and take them to the lady. This is a gesture of kindness and goodwill from the women to the new mom. They bring these foods to help the woman regain her strength and get back to her normal self. This brings about a connection between the women in that community and unites them.

Food is indeed a connector of people. If you want people to come to your party or do anything for you, just have food around, and you will be surprised how many will come through.

So, if you normally struggle with social connection, sharing your own home cooked meals can help you change that in a powerful way. When you see people enjoying your creation and giving you positive feedback, you will change your view of yourself. With the appreciation and admiration of your work, you will realize that your value and worth for yourself will increase.

It's Cheaper

Cooking at home helps you save money. When you cook at home, you tend to spend less than when you eat at a restaurant. The cost of ingredients tends to be lower than the price of food in restaurants. This, in turn, usually changes your overall financial situation in a positive way.

Money is one of the things that can really stress someone and bring a lot of pressure and conflict in relationships. In fact, a lot of couples are known to often argue about money. There have been terrible cases of partners killing their loved ones because of financial conflicts. For this reason, it is good to embrace home cooking as it is a good tool for cutting down on your budget. This will, therefore, help you and your partner save a bit of money and strengthen your relationship. This also helps make date nights more special in that you are not doing a routine.

It's Nourishing

Nutrition is very fundamental in keeping the brain healthy. This has been proven and emphasized a lot by several mental health organizations. In order to ensure that your brain remains healthy, nutrition should be a mainstream element of your mental health-care every single day. When you cook for yourself, you become more aware of the things that you are ingesting as well as how those things affect your body. With this knowledge, you will have the ability to be in more control of your diet and stay healthy.

When it comes to your mental and physical health, nutritious diets like fruits, legumes, dark leafy greens, and fish have been known to provide better outcomes. However, everybody's reaction to food is different. There are various physical influences, such as gut microbiomes and intolerances, that affect the different reactions of people to different foods. In order to ensure that you take care of your body and mental health in the best way possible, it is best that you use the best possible tool – cooking. It only requires proper timing.

While you may be too tired to cook and order take-out, it is worth noting that your mental health depends a lot on what you eat. Once you are in control of the food you eat, by cooking it, then you have a greater chance of having a very healthy brain and body.

There is less calorie consumption when you cook your own meals. Home cooked food tends to have low levels of carbohydrates, fat, and sugar than the food cooked in restaurants. This was proven to be true in the Public Health Nutrition journal, which was published in 2014.

Researchers in a national health and nutrition survey examined data that had been taken for four years. The data revealed that eight percent of adults who did not cook or cooked at least once a week usually took in 2,300 calories, 136 g of sugar, and 85 grams of fat in a day. These levels are all above the levels required.

In the meantime, almost 50% of people who made their own dinner every day or at least six times a week ate about 2,160 calories, 80 g of fat, and 120 g of sugar on a normal day. While it is still high, it is better than those who barely cook at home.

It Enables You to Have Control

Cooking ensures total control over your dishes. When making your own meals, you have more control over the amount of food you want, the ingredients you want to include in your meals, as well as the amount of salt. When you eat out, however, you give your control away to the chef who is going to cook the meal.

With this control, it is up to you to know and deal with your weight and food allergies as required. In case you are on a special diet because of a medical condition, cooking at home may also be the best option.

If you would like to eat your own food a lot more, you can invest in a slower cooker that would help you cook easily at home, as well as plastic containers that you would use to store leftovers in the fridge. You could also purchase a lunch box in which you could pack and carry your lunch in when going to work. This will help you avoid eating at your workplace and maintain your personal diet in a healthy way.

Cooking food at home also helps you help others with different food allergies. Maybe you have someone in your family who is allergic to a certain food, you could help them in a great way by cooking food at home. When you are in control of the diet, you will be able to help avoid the substance that the individual is allergic to.

Control in your kitchen through home cooking also helps you control the portion. In many fast food joints and restaurants, you will find much larger portions of food that are not necessary. This brings about a problem as you will be forced to consume all the food that you have bought.

However, when you make your own food, you can control the amount of food that you eat. This way, you will not need a random temptation to consume more food than you can handle.

It's Unifying

Cooking at home promotes unity. Yes, when you cook and eat together as a family, you and your family get the time to gather and bond. Members get to share their day's experiences with the rest of the family.

When a family eats together, there is a high likelihood that the children in the family will become healthy, both physically and mentally. This, in turn, causes them to perform better in school, become less obese, as well as reduces the likelihood of substance abuse.

Also, you can involve your kids in the cooking and bond with them during the activity. You could ask them to help clean some ingredients, read the recipe, or even check the oven when baking. This, as you will see, is a fun activity that would help you bond with your kids. Not only is it fun, but also a good platform to teach your kids healthy habits observed in eating. With this in mind, you will be motivated to make your own food at home and eat out less.

As you can now see, it is very fundamental that you prepare and cook your own food so that you may be healthy both mentally and physically.

If you have no idea what to cook, I will share a few recipes in the rest of the book that will help you have an idea of what you can do at home. I have included all sorts of foods from breakfast, lunches, appetizers, dinners, and many more. I hope you will enjoy them once you try them and will motivate you more to make your own cuisines.

BREAKFAST RECIPES

I have been trying out different recipes from my favorite restaurant for years. As I share some of my favorite recipes with you, I hope you will like them once you try them out.

How does your typical day begin? If you are like most adults, you probably snooze your alarm for a few minutes before you get up and get out of bed. Maybe you scroll your phone a bit to have a feel of what the social media has for you. Once you are out of bed, it is off to the day's events as you hasten to shower, get dressed, and probably drive to work or take a bus.

How about what you eat? Do you gobble down a bowl of oatmeal or cereals? Do you make a few pancakes, some eggs, or sausages? Do you try out a few pastries in the morning? This decision is very important.

Breakfast, which is the first meal of the day, is a fundamental meal for all individuals. When you eat breakfast, it means that you are breaking a fast that you have been through. Fasting means going without food. When you sleep at night, you are observing a fast because you are not eating anything. So when you wake up in the morning and eat a meal, you are breaking the night's fast, thus the name "breakfast."

So, is it true that breakfast is the most important meal? It could be you are wondering why people say that.

Well, nutritionists and doctors have, for years, agreed with these sentiments. They have always insisted that what you consume in the morning is very fundamental to your body as well as mental health. I tend to concur with them because when one wakes up in the morning, the physical state is different from when they slept. The fuel tank is usually lower in charge than the previous night or even empty. Just like any machine using gas cannot operate without fuel, it will be equally challenging for you to start and do your day's activities without your "fuel."

For this reason, it is very important to consider what you will fuel your body with. The food you eat is very important. Well, some find it okay to eat anything because it is better than eating nothing at all. However, it is best to plan your breakfast meals well and ensure that your body's fuel is healthy and beneficial to the body. Starting your day on a good meal even brighten up your day. A good start to your day will most likely bring about a good day.

For instance, you may choose to do some donuts or pastries for breakfast. While this is not bad, they are probably not the best foods to start your day with on a regular basis. They are very yummy and savory; however, their levels of calories, fats, and sugar are high, thus not healthy for regular consumption.

A balanced diet is the best way to go on about your breakfast. This is because a well-balanced diet usually gives you the nutrients that your body requires to get on with your day's activities. With a plate of a vast assortment of foods, you will be able to achieve a diet that is well-balanced for your body. For you to achieve this good diet, you will need a variety of foods like dairy products, veggies, proteins, fruits, and grains. In most cases, you will find most people taking eggs, whole-grain cereals, yogurt, pancakes, bacon, toast, toast, milk, juice, waffles, as well as fruits such as strawberries, mangoes, etc.

It is best to never skip breakfast, even if you are in a hurry to get to whatever place you are going. If you do so, your day may start on a low point, and you are likely to get very hungry as the day goes by. Due to hunger, you will be forced to overeat through the rest of the day. This is unhealthy and may bring health issues later in life. If you are in a hurry, grab something like some fresh fruit, a muffin, or even some yogurt, rather than skipping breakfast.

Below are some of my favorite recipes that you could try at home for breakfast. These recipes are very interesting to make and healthy. I hope you enjoy them.

IHOP's Bacon Temptation Omelet

I once went to IHOP for a breakfast meeting with a friend. I could not believe how delicious their omelet was. I had to check the menu once again to get the name right. The IHOP Bacon Temptation Omelet is so yummy. It is so fluffy and loaded with creamy cheese fillings and crispy bacon; this omelet is just perfect. Bacon lovers would love it!

Ingredients

3 Slices of American cheese

½ cup of Milk

1 cup of prepared pancake batter

3 Eggs

4 Cooked slices of bacon

1 cup shredded Monterey Jack cheese

Instructions

1. Preheat a skillet to 350 degrees.

2. Over medium heat melt the American cheese together with the milk in a small saucepan. Stir occasionally until the cheese melts and forms a cheese sauce. Once the cheese sauce is formed, simmer down the heat as much as you possibly can.

3. Combine the slices of bacon, eggs, milk, and the pancake batter in a medium bowl. Whisk them until they are well-combined. Spray some nonstick spray on the griddle and pour the omelet in. Form a rectangular shape and let the eggs cook as they form up.

4. When the eggs are nearly ready, pour the cheese sauce over the eggs. Fold the omelet into a roll, then top it up with more bacon and sprinkled cheese. If you have some leftover cheese sauce, you can serve the eggs with it on the side.

El Papi's Avocado Tomatillo Tacos

I love doing these green tacos on weekdays. I have made them so many times than I could count. These tacos usually have tortillas with tomatillo salsa, avocado, and spinach. One then tucks some scrambled eggs into the tortillas, and voila! Some delicious breakfast.

I got this from El Papi, one of the best tacos joints I know. They have become my family's breakfast routine for a long time. They are good for kids because they are deliciously combined with veggies that most kids avoid. You can sauté some spinach and also include some avocado, eggs, and a lot of fresh tomatillo salsa.

Ingredients

Extra-virgin olive oil, for brushing

Roasted Tomatillo Salsa, for serving

4 large eggs

5 charred or warmed tortillas

Freshly ground black pepper and sea salt, to taste

6 cups fresh spinach

1 sliced avocado

Microgreens (optional)

Lime wedges for serving (optional)

Sliced serrano peppers (optional)

Instructions

1. With the olive oil, lightly brush a nonstick skillet and heat to medium temperature. Take some spinach, put it in the skillet, and add a few pinches of pepper and salt. Sauté the spinach until it is wilted. If the spinach is too much, work in batches.

2. Once the spinach is ready, take them out of the pan and place it on a plate. Wipe out the skillet as you prepare to cook the eggs.

3. Lightly brush the skillet again with olive oil and let it heat to medium temperature. Scramble the eggs and add them to the skillet. Allow them to cook for a few seconds, stir, and then scramble the eggs again until they are set.

4. Combine the tacos with the sautéed spinach, eggs, slices of avocado, and scoops of tomatillo salsa. Top up with some sliced serranos and microgreens.

5. Serve with lime wedges, if you like.

Denny's Pancake Puppies

I do not know if you have had a taste of these puppies. Found at Denny's, these are the only breakfast appetizer. I have ever tasted. Yes, breakfast appetizer. That is what Denny's calls these yummy small pancakes. I believe they are a mix of both beignets and funnel cakes.

If you are a frequent customer at Denny's, you have probably come across them. They are small and ball-shaped, fried in vegetable oil. They are more like a beignet, funnel cake, or donut.

Though most people would prefer to have these as dessert, Denny's Restaurant usually serves them as a breakfast dish.

They are so yummy. I hope you will get the best of them from this copycat recipe.

Ingredients

Pancake mix (Preferably one that you will only need to water to add)

A cup of water

Oil

Instructions

1. Heat the vegetable oil to medium heat.

2. Combine pancake mixture and water in a medium-sized bowl and stir until it blends well.

3. Drop the batter into the oil using a cookie scoop and cook until it is brown at the bottom. Flip it over and fry for an extra 45 seconds.

4. Take it out of the oil and drain the extra oil. If you like, sprinkle some powdered sugar to sweeten.

5. Serve with maple syrup.

The Grand Lux Café's Chicken-N-Waffles

I once visited my sister in New York City, and, being the foodie I am, I sampled foods from various places. That is when I had my first experience at the Grand Lux Cafe.

A sister restaurant to the Cheesecake Factory, Grand Lux Cafe, gave my palate one of the best brunches I have ever tasted - chicken and waffles.

Ingredients

For the chicken tenders:

2 teaspoons ground black pepper

4 cups all-purpose flour

1 teaspoon salt

3 pounds chicken tenders

2 teaspoons seasoned salt

4 cups buttermilk

For the waffles:

3 teaspoons vegetable oil

1 packet active dry yeast

4 large egg white (divided use)

4 large egg yolks

2 cups lukewarm water

2 teaspoon almond extract

2 cups whole milk

5 ounces of melted and cooled butter

3/4 cup sugar and 1 teaspoon (divided use)

4 cups sifted all-purpose flour

3 teaspoons vanilla extract

1/2 teaspoon salt

vegetable oil

<u>For sweetened butter:</u>

2 tablespoon powdered sugar

5 ounces butter

Instructions

Waffles:

1. Dissolve 1 teaspoon of sugar and the yeast in the lukewarm water. Give it about 5 to 10 minutes to stand. You will know the yeast is getting ready when it starts to form bubbles and foam.

2. Put the flour and salt in a large bowl and stir. In another medium-sized bowl, mix the yeast batter with the remaining portion of sugar, one egg white, and 3 egg yolks. Stir for them to blend well. When well-blended, add the rest of the water, the melted butter, almond extract, oil, milk, and vanilla. Beat until the mixture becomes creamy and buttery.

3. Pour in the liquid batter in the flour mixture and whisk to make it smooth. In a clean bowl, whisk the remaining egg whites. Ensure that the bowl is clean so that the egg whites can properly fluff up. Whip until you see stiff peaks forming.

4. Gently pour the egg whites into the batter and give it about an hour to stand for 1 hour. Check and keep stirring after every 20 minutes.

5. On medium heat, preheat your waffle maker, then scoop the batter and place it on the waffle maker. To spread the mixture over the waffle iron, you may need to use a spatula that is heatproof. Close the waffle maker and cook until the waffle is ready. Your waffle iron is most likely to notify you when it is ready, as most usually have an indicator for that purpose.

Chicken tenders:

1. Preheat the vegetable oil in a deep fryer to 350 degrees F. stir together the pepper, flour, salt, seasoned salt in a medium bowl.

2. In a baking dish, pour in buttermilk. Dab the chicken tenders with a paper towel to dry. Dip every chicken tender in the seasoned flour, shake off the extra flour, then dredge in the buttermilk.

3. Put it back into the seasoned flour, shake off the excess flour, then put them on a wire rack for later. Give them about 5 minutes to rest before you cook them. This will help make the crust crunchy.

4. Fry the chicken tender for 5 to 6 minutes, only a few at a time. Fry until they turn golden brown. Keep checking the tenders and turning them after about 3 to 4 minutes. This, however, depends on how deep the oil is. Once they are ready, place on a clean wire rack and allow them to cool.

Sweetened butter:

1. Melt the butter gently in a small saucepan over low heat. Pour in the powdered sugar and mix.

2. Serve warm.

Note: To serve this dish, set a waffle on a plate, then top it with the chicken tenders. Sprinkle some powdered sugar, then serve with the sweetened butter.

IHOP's Banana Pancakes

As a lover of banana bread, I have come to love banana pancakes so much. They are made with whole wheat flour and oat and are very healthy and delicious. When I leave home in a hurry sometimes, I like to pass by IHOP, which is along the way to my office. My taste buds just marvel at the blend of flavors in the pancake. So, I made my own copycat recipe.

My husband and kids love them too, so we mostly make them on Saturdays. My kids normally eat too many of them, thus the need for ample time to make them.

With ripe bananas around your house, you can try this banana pancake recipe and have a feel of the sweetness I am talking about. It is one super easy recipe that will surely make your regular weekend breakfast much more interesting.

Bananas are naturally very sweet. However, I find them sweeter when included in bread or muffins. They are so sweet and very suitable for vegans.

For wholesome breakfast pancakes, I normally use a mix of whole wheat pastry flour and oat flour. The mix makes them nicely fluffy and light. I then add in a bit of nutmeg, vanilla, and cinnamon. I then add plenty of ripe bananas, which make them very sweet, thus no need for sweeteners. This, however, does not limit you from using maple syrup.

Ingredients

Ground flaxseed

½ cup of Water

Mashed banana (about 1 large)

Extra-virgin olive oil (Including extra for brushing)

1 tsp. Vanilla

½ cup Almond milk

1 cup Whole wheat pastry flour

½ cup Oat flour

1 tbsp Baking powder

1 tsp Baking soda

½ tsp Cinnamon

½ tsp Nutmeg

Pinch of Sea salt

Pecans, slices of banana, and maple syrup for serving

Instructions

1. Combine the water, banana, and flaxseed in a large bowl. Smash and mix until well-combined. Let the mix sit for 5 minutes for it until it is thick. Add the almond milk, vanilla, and olive oil, and whisk.

2. In the mixture, add in the flour and sprinkle the baking soda, baking powder, nutmeg, cinnamon, and salt. Mix until all the ingredients are well-combined, but the dough a bit lumpy. Ensure that the batter is not too thick. If it is, stir in an extra tablespoon of almond milk.

3. Heat a griddle or nonstick skillet to medium heat and on it, brush in a little olive oil. With a measuring cup, pour in the batter into the pan and use the cup's back to gently spread the batter evenly on the pan. Let it cook until air-bubbles appear. This could be about 1½ minutes on each side.

4. Simmer down the heat as required to keep the middle part of the pancake from burning. Normally, I begin cooking the pancakes on medium heat then move to low. It is good to maintain the heat at an averagely low since, with time, the pan gets to have some residual heat after every batch.

5. Serve the pancakes with sliced bananas and maple syrup. You could also top it off with a few pecans if you so desire.

McDonald's Egg White Delight

You have probably seen Egg McMuffins at McDonald's. I love to grab some when I leave home in a hurry and have no time to make breakfast. Well, there is an easier and healthier version of them - the egg white delight. With this copycat recipe, you can make something closer to the McMuffins, but with fewer calories.

Besides being low on calories, the egg white delight from McDonald's is very satisfying for breakfast and high on fiber from the English wheat muffin. So, save yourself some cash by using this recipe to make the Egg McMuffin's cousin.

Ingredients

Wheat English Muffins (as many as you'd like to serve)

Slices of Canadian Bacon (one per English muffin)

Egg whites (one egg white per English muffin)

Salt and pepper to taste

White Cheddar cheese (one slice per English muffin)

Instructions

1. In a toaster, toast the English wheat muffins.

2. Heat the Canadian bacon in a small skillet until it is heated through and turns light brown. When ready, remove it from the skillet and set aside.

3. Break the eggs and separate the egg whites from the yolks. Whisk the egg whites together vigorously.

4. Spray a little of non-stick spray in a skillet. Pour the egg whites into it, then simmer down the heat. Cook the egg whites slowly and season with pepper and salt. Once the egg whites are well-cooked, make the sandwiches.

5. Cut the egg whites into the portions you prefer. Place the pieces at the base of the English muffins. Top each egg muffins with a slice of cheese. Add a slice of Canadian bacon on each of the muffins then finish with the bun.

Danny's Donuts French Toast

A lot of people have eaten the French toast at Danny's Donuts. Many have admitted that it is the French toast they love most. Well, you will be glad to know that you can recreate this great French toast at home.

Ingredients

Texas Toast bread (two slices per serving)

Powdered sugar to taste for garnish

1 cup Milk

Pinch of Salt

2 Eggs

½ cup All-purpose flour

1 tsp. Vanilla

Instructions

1. Beat the milk and eggs together in a medium-sized bowl. Next, whisk in the powdered sugar, salt, flour,

and vanilla into the egg batter. Filter the mixture of custard into another bowl with a wire mesh strainer.

2. Heat a griddle to around 350 degrees then brush it with butter. Put the bread into the mixture of custard, flip it over, and then put it on the heated cooking surface. Let it cook for a couple of minutes per side. When cooked through, the bread will turn golden.

3. Remove the bread from the skillet. Diagonally cut the toast, sprinkle some powdered sugar on it, then use butter as the last topping.

McDonald's Ham and Egg Sandwiches

McDonald's Egg McMuffins inspire me. You can make up a lot of dishes inspired by the famous McDonald's delicacy.

Well, with a few ingredients like avocado, some mayo, salsa, and even ketchup, I made the traditional breakfast sandwiches yummier than ever. These are not only meant for breakfast, but you could have them for dinner as well.

They are so quick to fix - about 30 to 45 minutes.

Ingredients

Melted butter

1 cup Shredded cheddar cheese

1 cup Finely chopped ham (fully cooked)

Pinch Coarsely ground pepper

2 tbsp Melted butter

½ cup Milk

Prepackaged Baking mix/biscuit mix

2 Eggs (per serving)

Coarsely ground pepper

1 cup Shredded cheddar cheese

½ cup Milk

Salt

Avocado, salsa, red onion and sliced tomato (Optional toppings)

Instructions

1. Preheat the oven to 450.

2. Mix the cheese, biscuit mix, pepper, and ham in a large bowl. Gently pour in some milk and mix until it is well moist.

3. Find a surface, lightly flour it and gently knead some dough for 10 times. Roll out the dough to a thickness of 1 inch then cut into portions using a biscuit cutter.

4. On an ungreased baking sheet, place the cut pieces then brush over the melted butter. Sprinkle the

leftover pepper then bake for 15 minutes when they will have turned golden brown.

5. As they bake, prepare the eggs by whisking them in a bowl together with salt, pepper, and milk. Heat the butter in a large nonstick skillet over medium heat. Pour the egg mixture in and let it cook. Keep stirring until the eggs become thick, and there is no more liquid egg. Add in the cheese then transfer from the heat.

6. Cut the warm biscuits into two halves. On the bottom, place the egg mixture and toppings as you like then place the other top.

Fast Food Alternative Overnight Oats

All oatmeal lovers would love this recipe and find these overnight oats to be a perfect breakfast. I have tasted all sorts of oatmeal dishes in lots of restaurants, thanks to my busy life. Wendy's, Chic-Fill-A – so many restaurants have this dish in many kinds of ways. It is best for people who rarely have time to prepare breakfast before heading out. So, I made my own.

This recipe basically includes whole rolled oats soaked overnight in almond milk. I also occasionally top up a dash of maple syrup. Oats are so good to consume in the morning since they are light and easy for digestion. The oatmeal mix also has a full consistency that is like porridge, which is very satisfying.

With a few toppings, overnight oats could make such a luscious meal that you would, most definitely, take over and over again. They can be a great way to make your breakfast routine a little spicier.

You can experiment with all sorts of stuff from your favorite jam, seeds, nuts, butter, and fruits, as toppings.

A few of each category include:

Fresh Fruit: Bananas, blackberries, strawberries, blueberries, Raspberries.

Dried Fruits: Raisins, apricots, coconut, cranberries, cherries

Spices: Pumpkin Pie Spice, vanilla, cinnamon, nutmeg

Nuts and Seeds: Walnuts, almonds, chia seeds, pecans, peanut butter, pumpkin Seeds, Almond Butter

Creamy stuff: Half n Half, Almond milk, cream, milk

Sweet Things: Brown sugar, chocolate chips, stevia, caramel, Agave Nectar, berry jam, honey, real Maple Syrup.

You can add other toppings that you would like to add. The ingredients above are just a few of the toppings you may use.

Ingredients

1 cup Whole rolled oats

Maple syrup to taste

1 cup Light coconut milk or Almond milk

Preferred toppings

Sea salt

Instructions

1. Mix the oats, maple syrup, coconut milk or almond, and salt in a small jar and stir. Leave it to chill overnight.

2. In the morning, put the oats in a bowl, and mix in more coconut milk or almond for consistency, if desired.

3. Top with the toppings you desire.

4. Another option would be to mix up the overnight oats with the toppings in containers the night before.

Notes: If you are vegan, you could replace honey with maple syrup.

Dunkin Donuts Chocolate Chip Muffins

My daughter Christie loves Dunkin Donuts' Chocolate Chip muffins. Whenever we pass by the restaurant to pick up a few snacks, she must have one. So, I decided to bring this yumminess home to her. I also decided to make them myself to lower the calories that Chocolate Chip muffins at Dunkin Donuts have. With me making these at home, I can be able to control the number of calories.

It is always expected that when I bake these, they should be a big batch. My family loves them so much; I have to make so many of them for them to feel satisfied. With kids in the house, this is a snack that you want to make a large batch because they are most likely to love them so much.

These are a great start to the day as they are sweet and full of flavor. With mini chocolate chips, these muffins are soft and fluffy. You would be surprised how fast kids can gobble them up. To make them more healthy, they have whole wheat flour, Greek yogurt, and a little maple syrup. You do not have to worry about the refined sugar or hydrogenated oils. These muffins lack such junk.

They are easy to cook and take about 25-30 minutes.

Ingredients

1 Egg

3 tbsp Honey, or maple syrup

1 cup Plain Greek yogurt

1 tsp Vanilla extract

1/3 cup Extra virgin olive oil or mashed avocado

¾ cup Milk

2 cups Whole wheat flour

Cooking spray

3 tsp Aluminum-free baking powder

1 cup Mini chocolate chips

3 tsp Baking soda

Instructions

1. With the oven preheating at 425 degrees, spray the cooking spray on a non-stick muffin tin and set aside.

2. Whisk the egg for a few seconds in a large mixing bowl. In it, add milk, maple syrup, yogurt, baking soda, baking powder, oil, vanilla, and whisk to combine.

3. Add in flour and stir gently until it is well combined with the mix. The batter will most likely be thick. Avoid over-mixing as it will make the muffins tough. Sprinkle the chocolate chips and do a few more gentle stirs.

4. With an ice cream scoop, place the batter into the twelve openings and bake for 6 minutes. Decrease the heat to 375 degrees F and bake for extra 8-10 minutes. To find out if they are ready, you can insert a toothpick or fork at the center. If it comes out clean, then the muffins are ready.

5. Remove them from the oven, and let them cool for around 5 minutes. After the 5 minutes, move them to a cooling rack to completely cool off.

Note: These muffins are best cooked with whole plain Greek yogurt as they make the muffins moister than when you use 0% Greek yogurt. It is also so much more salutary than the non-fat. Take your time to find and purchase it now.

For the muffins to stay for about 2-5 days, store in a cool, dry place. If you would like them to stay for months (at the most 3 months), store them in a freezer.

APPETIZER RECIPES

An appetizer is some sort of a tease-dish of a particular meal. It can be in the form of food or drinks, which may also range from soft drinks to alcoholic drinks. A few examples of appetizers include; cheese, crackers, salad, shrimp, potato skins, cocktail, bruschetta, calamari, and mussels. They are provided in some restaurants while others find them too elegant.

An appetizer, better known as an hors d'oeuvre, is intended to spur your appetite and increase your craving for the meal.

The word literally means a dish that appetizes or whets the appetite.

Since appetizers are usually intriguing, they make it possible for the diner to savor foods that are too heavy to be consumed in larger portions or too pronounced in flavor.

Appetizers are the most enjoyable portion of a meal. Of the appetizers that I have tried, below are a few of them that I find it easy to cook and delicious. I bet you will find several that will make you embrace having appetizers more often. Enjoy!

Texas Roadhouse Rolls and Cinnamon Butter

Every time I think of Texas Roadhouse Rolls, I think of my husband. He loves the place so much. The waiters at the Roadhouse in our state know him. They know his usual dish. When I go with him, I go for the rolls with cinnamon butter, which are so yummy, right from the oven. Nothing beats that! It brings a little bit of heaven on earth. They can be very addictive.

So, since I was hooked, I created a copycat dish that was also quite delicious. Now I get to eat them more often at home.

Ingredients

100 degrees warm water

½ cup Softened butter

1 Egg

½ cup Milk

1 packet Active dry yeast

½ tsp Salt

2 tbsp Melted butter

3 cups Flour

2 tbsp Sugar

Cinnamon Butter Ingredients

1 tbsp Honey

1 Softened butter stick (1/2 cup butter)

2 tbsp Powdered sugar (or to taste)

½ tbsp Cinnamon

Instructions

1. On the stove, heat the milk to 180 degrees in a pot. You can also use a safe bowl to heat it in the microwave.

2. Take the milk from the heat and put the butter in it. Allow it to cool to 115 degrees.

3. Put the yeast and sugar in warm water and let it dissolve. Give it about 5 minutes to sit.

4. Add the milk, cup of flour, sugar, yeast, and salt in a stand mixer bowl. Use a paddle attachment or which to combine.

5. Add an egg in and beat until well-combined.

6. Pour in a couple more cups of flour, scraping down the sides as you add and mix one at a time.

7. Turn on the dough hook and put in ½ cup of flour at low speed a little at a time. Do this until the dough forms and does not stick on the sides. Knead it with the dough hook for 3 to 5 minutes until it becomes soft.

8. Brush a large bowl with cooking spray or oil.

9. Dust the counter lightly with flour then turn the dough out. To ensure that the dough does not stick to your hands, dust some flour on your hands before you turn.

10. Make the dough ball-like and put it in a greased bowl.

11. Turn the dough in the greased pot once to ensure both sides of the dough are oiled. Cover it and let it set in a warm, dry place for at least an hour, when it becomes

double in size. Sometimes, I place it in the oven and turn on the inside light.

12. When the dough is ready, place it on a well-floured surface, then with a dusted rolling pin, roll it out to half an inch thick. Cut it into dough rectangles using a pizza cutter or a dough scraper. These can be about 2x3 inches.

13. Fold the rectangles with the short edges under and coming together in the middle. This will make a round shape at the top.

14. Put it on a cookie sheet that is lightly greased, cover, and give it about 20 minutes to sit until it doubles.

15. Preheat the oven to 350 degrees F.

16. Bake the rolls at 350 degrees F for 10-14 minutes until they turn to a deep golden brown. Take them out of the oven and brush over the melted butter.

17. Serve it warm together with the cinnamon butter.

Fat Ronnie's Deep-Fried Mushrooms

I first tasted this dish at Fat Ronnie's, and I have to admit that these deep-fried mushrooms are some of the yummiest mushrooms I have ever eaten in a restaurant. With different feels in one, these mushrooms please the palate with their crispy and crunchy outside and the tenderness on the inside. If you have never done these before, do not worry. It is a very easy process - easier than you think. They are also fast to make in just a few minutes.

You can make these mushrooms for your friends at a party or a family dinner with your loved ones. You can also use it as a side dish when doing other dishes like fish.

Ingredients

Vegetable oil for frying

1 teaspoon Baking Powder

3 cups Flour

1 cup Buttermilk

2 teaspoons salt

10 ounces washed, dried fresh Mushrooms (with stems removed)

1 teaspoon Ground Pepper

Instructions

1. Heat the vegetable oil to 375 degrees.

2. In a bowl, mix some flour, baking powder, salt, and pepper.

3. Put the buttermilk in a bowl.

4. Dip the mushrooms into the seasoned flour, shake off the excess flour then dip the floured mushrooms in the buttermilk.

5. Glaze the mushrooms with the buttermilk then shake off excess buttermilk.

6. Put the mushrooms into the seasoned flour once again, then shake off the extra buttermilk.

7. Cook the mushrooms until they are golden brown for about 1 to 2 minutes. Ensure that you stir and flip the mushrooms over for both sides to be cooked.

8. On a wire, drain mushrooms and let them rest on a bar pan.

Note: In case your buttermilk thicken more that you desire, you can add a few tablespoons of water for it to become lighter.

Olive Garden Spinach Artichoke Dip

I tasted this for the first time at Olive Garden. I bet a lot of people love Olive Garden because it is always packed, especially on the weekend. If you would like to go grab a dish, you better get there early. I love to go there often for birthdays or large family gatherings. So, what makes the Spinach Artichoke Dip at Olive Garden so unique?

Well, in my opinion, it could be the several distinct kinds of cheese that they use in their sauce that makes it so yummy. They normally use Asiago, Mozzarella, Parmesan, Cream Cheese, and Romano, which, when combined together, bring out a savory sauce that anyone would love.

Ingredients

2 cups of milk

5 ounces frozen and chopped spinach

1 cup shredded Parmesan cheese

2 shredded tablespoon Romano cheese

1 cup shredded Mozzarella

1/2 cup artichokes diced marinated artichokes

4 tablespoons butter

1 teaspoon salt

4 tablespoons flour

1/2 teaspoon black pepper

1 teaspoon chopped garlic

1 tablespoon shredded Asiago cheese

3 tablespoons cream cheese

1/2 cup Mozzarella cheese for the top

Instructions

1. Heat the butter to melt over medium heat, n a medium-sized saucepan. Add the flour into the melted butter and let it cook until the sauce becomes fragrant for 2 to 4 minutes. Top up with the cup of cold milk, then stir until the sauce thickens. Sprinkle some salt and pepper to season.

2. Add in some diced artichokes, Parmesan cheese, spinach, Asiago cheese, Romano cheese, garlic, cream

cheese, Mozzarella cheese, into the saucepan, and stir until the mixture is warm enough.

3. Pour the dip into a dish that is oven-proof then sprinkle the Mozzarella cheese on top. Set the dip under the broiler in an oven. Cook until the dip's top starts to turn to brown.

Applebee's Veggie Patch Pizza

In my restaurant adventures, I once popped in at Applebee's for lunch. I loved the dish, but one thing that stood out for me was Veggie Patch Pizza, aka the Crescent Roll Vegetarian Pizza. It is such a yummy appetizer that everyone would love. With the flakey crescent roll pastry, the creamy Ranch Dressing, and the Fresh veggies, no one would want to miss out on this yumminess. They are perfect for parties.

If you are a vegetarian, this dish is just for you. You could make it for your friends at the pot-lucks or tailgate parties. Just about anywhere where there are hungry people.

Veggie lovers, here we go. This cold dish has tomatoes, carrots, broccoli, zucchini, bell peppers, and squash. But, you can drop any veggie you like into it, and it will come out just right. Consider the vegetables you love to eat raw together with the ranch dip and use them as toppings however you like. You can also use the veggies that have been in your kitchen for a while.

Ingredients

1 tbsp. Olive oil

1 cup Fresh Shredded Parmesan cheese

Diced onions (to taste)

Diced mushrooms (to taste)

Diced tomato (to taste)

1 tbsp Italian seasoning

2 Minced cloves garlic

1 cup (or more) Shredded mozzarella cheese

Pepper and salt to taste

Flour tortillas (one per serving)

Spinach artichoke dip (from the previous recipe)

Instructions

1. Sauté the onion and diced mushrooms in a hot saucepan. Ensure that the oil is enough to cover the pan at the bottom. Season with the pepper and salt and let them cook until they are tender and light brown in color. Add the minced garlic and cook while stirring for another extra 2 minutes.

2. Brush some oil on the tortilla and put them on a large pan or griddle to cook. Ensure that both sides are well-cooked and light brown. Take them out of the baking sheet and set aside. Do the same for all tortillas.

3. Evenly spread the artichoke dip and spinach on each tortilla. Spread them within half an inch from the edge. Add the onion and cooked mushroom, then the diced tomatoes. Sprinkle the mozzarella cheese evenly on the pizzas and let it cook until the cheese melts at 350. Finish by sprinkling the shredded Parmesan cheese.

4. Slice the pizza into wedges and serve.

Note: In case you make too much spinach artichoke dip, you can put the rest in a casserole dish and bake for about 30 minutes at 350. You can also store it in the fridge for the next time you make the pizza.

Wingstop Garlic Parmesan Wings

I love going to Wingstop for their wings. The Garlic Parmesan Wings are particularly the ones that take me there. They are my favorite Wingstop dishes. If you love hot and spicy stuff, well, this is for you. These chicken wings are just yum!

Ingredients

2 lbs. Chicken wings

½ cup Parmesan cheese

1 tsp Cayenne pepper

2 tsp. Garlic powder

Pinch Ground black pepper

Pinch Seasoned salt

About 1 cup of All-purpose flour

2 tbsp. Butter

Parsley for garnish - Optional

Instructions

1. Preheat the oven to 360 degrees.

2. Mix the all-purpose flour, ground black pepper, cayenne pepper, and seasoned salt in a bowl.

3. Cut the chicken wings and dip them in the flour.

4. In a large pot, or deep fryer, heat some oil to 350 degrees. Deep fry the wings for roughly 6 to 8 minutes, then remove and set on a wire rack to drain. You can fry several wings at the same time, depending on the size of your pot. Ensure that you stir at least once to ensure even cooking of the wings.

5. Cook the wings until they turn to brown then bake until the chicken is well-cooked or for about 20 minutes.

6. For the sauce, melt the butter plus the garlic powder in a pan.

7. Once the wings are ready, remove the wings from the oven and put them in a large bowl.

8. Into the melted butter, stir in half a portion of the Parmesan cheese then pour the molten garlic butter

on the wings. Toss them until the wings are well-coated with the molten garlic butter.

9. Sprinkle the rest of the Parmesan cheese on top of the wings and serve.

Notes: When cutting the wings, divide them into three parts: the "drummette," the wing, and the wingtip. Well, the wingtip is the piece at the outer most end of the wing. Quite explanatory. These pieces are good for making chicken broth, so save them up for that purpose. Once you have removed the tip and are remaining with the "drummette" and the wing, cut the two from the joint. The joint is downward from where you will cut the wingtip. Once you cut the joint, you will remain with the two pieces that you will use for the dish.

The sauce is best with chopped garlic rather than the garlic powder.

For the butter sauce, you can use another alternative where you chop the garlic to fair fineness then heat in butter for around 6 to 8 minutes. It is best if you simmer the garlic to tenderness until it produces some wonderful spicy fragrance. After, add in the Parmesan cheese. When you use fresh garlic, you give the sauce a deeper dimension that everybody would appreciate.

Unlike other dishes, I would advise that you use the canned Parmesan cheese. This is because it gives the wings a flakier coating and helps retain its form.

When you make these garlic parmesan wings, make just enough for one serving. This is because the wings do not turn out well when reheated. Reheating causes the wings to be way softer and a bit soggy.

Hooters Hot Wings

Have you ever had the hot wings at Hooters? I am not exaggerating when I say that these wings are different from the usual ones. Hooters make them different from the normal wings. They batter their wings instead of frying them like most other wings. This adds some crispiness to the outer part of the wings. They turn out more flavored, crispier, and of course, yummier!

Ingredients

2 lbs. Chicken wings with the wing and drumette parts

1 cup All-purpose flour

1 tsp Paprika

½ cup Whole wheat flour

Salt

Teaspoon cayenne pepper

Instructions

1. Mix the flours, paprika, cayenne pepper, and salt in a large mixing bowl. Ensure that you blend them well.

2. Cut the chicken wings into flippers and drumettes, then wash and drain.

3. In the flour mixture, coat the chicken wings then chill for about 1 hour and 30 minutes.

4. Once the chicken wings are ready to cook, heat the oil. When the oil is eventually hot, put in the pieces of chicken pieces. Do not put in so many of them at the same time to give each of them proper space to cook. Fry them until they turn golden brown. When ready, remove from the oil and place them on a drying rack to drain.

5. When all wings are ready, put them in a large bowl. Pour in the hot sauce batter and mix them nicely.

6. Transfer the chicken wings from the bowl to a serving platter using some tongs or a fork.

7. Serve instantly. (Give your guests a lot of paper towels. The chicken wings may be too oily.)

Note: If you like, you can serve the chicken wings together with the blue cheese you love as dressing.

Olive Garden Lasagna Dip and Pasta Chips

I have been to Olive Garden several times. With my family and sometimes with my friends. Lasagna at Olive Garden makes a day more glorious, especially when shared with those you love.

This delicacy is stuffed with beef, cheese, and creamy and savory tomato sauce smothered in it. You will stop missing the milling salsa.

Prepare the chips and dip before the lasagna so that when the lasagna is ready, you can serve it piping hot.

Looking for a place to take your family? Try Olive Garden and have a taste of their Lasagna and pasta dip. You and your family will have an awesome casual family meal like no other.

Ingredients

1 package Lasagna noodles

1 tsp Garlic salt

Oil for frying

1 lbs. Ground beef

1 lbs. Ground Italian sausage

1 small (about 16 oz) jar of Marinara sauce

1 cup Shredded Mozzarella cheese

1 tbsp Italian seasoning

½ cup freshly Shredded Parmesan cheese

1 cup. Ricotta cheese

Instructions

1. Cook the flat lasagna noodles in a large pot of boiling salted water until al dente. When ready, drain pasta the pasta noodles and be careful not to tear.

2. Preheat a skillet with a little oil to 360 degrees.

3. Put a few lasagna noodles carefully in the hot oil and let it cook until it is crispy and golden brown. Remove the noodles from the hot oil and place them on a wire rack to drain and cool. Sprinkle some garlic salt immediately.

Note: Cook the noodles in small batches until they are all cooked.

1. For the dip, preheat the oven to 370 degrees.

2. Cook the ground beef and the Italian ground sausage in a large saucepan over medium. Cook until the meat turns brown. Break the meat into small pieces as you cook. When ready, drain the meat and put it back into the saucepan.

3. Add some Marinara sauce to add to the sweetness of the meats then season with Italian seasoning. Heat it for about 5 minutes then simmer in 10 minutes.

4. Build the dip in an iron skillet or a deep casserole dish and place half the sauce at the bottom of the pan. At the bottom of the dish, spread the ricotta cheese. On top of the ricotta, spread half of the Mozzarella cheese then add the rest of the sauce on the mozzarella cheese.

5. Add the rest of the parmesan cheese topping and let to cook for roughly 30 minutes. You can also put it in the oven to make the cheese brown if you desire.

6. Serve the dip together with the pasta chips.

Cheddars Scratch Kitchen Cheese Fries

Yum! My mouth is already watering when I reminisce about this savory dish. Cheddars Scratch Kitchen is where I have had the best of these. They make lots of other delicious appetizers that I am a big fan of. Every time I pay them a visit, I have to have a taste of their Texas Cheese Fries. You do not know what you are missing if your teeth have not dug into these French fries coated with bacon and cheese.

Cheddars Scratch Kitchen is an awesome place to be. They make all their food in-house, from scratch. A lot of people from all over the country request the Texas Cheese Fries from Cheddars.

I just love how plenty the bacon and cheese are—one of the tastiest comfort foods I have had. I am starting to crave it as I write.

Ingredients

1 bag of Frozen French fries (regular-cut)

Vegetable oil for frying

Thin-sliced bacon (to taste)

Ranch Salad Dressing

1 cup. Shredded Cheddar-Jack cheese blend

Instructions

1. Preheat the oven to 420 degrees.

2. In a deep saucepan, pour about 4 inches of vegetable oil. Heat the oil to 345 degrees. Prepare the fries as instructed on the package. If your deep fryer is small, fry in small batches. Fry them until they turn crisp and golden. When ready, remove the fries from the saucepan and set them on a wire rack to cool.

3. In a skillet, cook the bacon over medium heat until they turn brown and al dente. Place them on paper towels to dry.

4. Put the ready French fries into an ovenproof dish. Ensure that you leave a well in the middle where you will put the container of ranch dressing.

5. Add the pieces of bacon and shredded cheese then place in the already-hot oven for 6 to 9 minutes. Once the cheese melts and turns brown, the dish is ready. Remove it from the oven. In the middle of the fries, place a small bowl of Ranch dressing.

LUNCH RECIPES

Many a time, people forgo their lunch on most days. Sometimes I don't get to eat lunch when I'm busy. We all have different reasons why we do that. Some are trying to lose weight, while others are too busy. However, no matter the reason, skipping lunch is a bad habit that we should all avoid. Lunch is very important, and we should all ensure that we take it, no matter how little.

When we eat, we get energy from the food that we have consumed. Therefore, when we have lunch, the food raises the level of our blood sugar during the day, enabling us to focus more as we push through the day.

When it comes to losing weight, studies have proven that people who skip lunch tend to gain even more weight. This is because, by dinner time, they are usually hungry, thus eat more than they are supposed to. They eat more to compensate for the lunch that they missed.

It is very important that kids have lunch every day. This is because the lunch provides them with the nutrients and vitamins that they need for the day. Without the nutrients, kids are prone to suffer low productivity in their physical and mental selves.

People are becoming busier by the day in this fast-paced world. We spend so much time rushing through our schedule and missing lunch. Some assume that taking a break is a waste of time. However, breaks are very important and great opportunities to recharge our batteries. When you eat lunch, you can be assured that you are helping your body and mind to stay healthy, as is required.

Below are a few copycat recipes that I love to make at home.

Wendy's Grilled Chicken Sandwich

My best friend, Catie, is a lover of sandwiches. Since she is always in a hurry, she loves buying them at restaurants so she can have them at the office or when she is in transit between meetings. So, she went to Wendy's Southwest and had their Avocado Chicken Sandwich. She could not stop talking about it. Knowing I am a foodie, she shared her palatal delight when we met. I had to try that dish. She made it look so yummy.

So, I put all these ingredients together in an impulse and voila, I got some delicious sandwich, almost like the one Catie had told me about.

If you are constantly in a hurry, moving from place to place, just throw the bacon in the microwave for a few minutes, then assemble the toast. It is really easy and takes around 30 minutes.

You can carry it in a paper towel, which will help keep the sandwich from making a mess.

Ingredients

Split Kaiser rolls or ciabatta (one per serving)

1 tbsp Italian salad dressing mix

Halved boneless skinless chicken breasts (one half per serving)

1 Peeled ripe avocado, sliced thinly

1 tbsp Mayonnaise

1 Slices of pepper jack cheese (per serving)

Halved bacon strips to taste

Deli coleslaw (pre-prepared)

Dijon mustard to taste

Sliced tomato, one per serving

Instructions

1. Using a meat mallet, pound the chicken to make it flat then sprinkle the dressing mix on both sides.

2. On an oiled grill, broil the chicken, over medium heat, covered. Cook each side for 5 to 7 minutes. Put some cheese on the chicken and continue to grill it, covered, for an extra 2 minutes or longer until the cheese melts.

3. Cut the rolls in halves and grill them with the cut sides down. Do this for around 2 minutes until the rolls are toasted.

4. Mix the mustard and mayonnaise then spread on top of the roll. Cover the bottom of the roll with bacon, chicken, coleslaw, avocado, and tomato then place the other tops.

Chipotle Burrito Bowls

I love going to Chipotle. I know I am not the only one. I sometimes crave it!

Chipotle's chicken or guacamole is just out of this world. If I could, I would have my lunches there twice a week. These guys are also everywhere, always tempting me to have a bite there every time. There is one near my neighborhood, and I often find myself there.

The burrito bowls are amazing. I had to find a way to have them all the time without spending a lot of money. Well, this is what I came up with.

Ingredients

1 lbs. Boneless, skinless chicken thighs

Pinch Black pepper

2 tsp Garlic powder

2 tsp Ground cumin

1 tsp Chili powder

1 tbsp Dried onions

Vegetable oil

1 tsp Dried oregano

1 tbsp Lime juice

1 small bag Defrosted corn

Pepper and salt to taste

½ cup Diced red onion

1 cup White rice

Instructions

1. In a Ziploc bag that is gallon-sized, place your chicken thighs and some oil and seal it. Start tossing and turning the chicken in the bag until the oil is well-coated on them.

2. In a small bowl, combine all the seasonings then pour them in the bag with chicken. Seal it once again and toss until all of the chicken in the bag is nicely glazed with the seasoning mix. Place the chicken bag in the fridge and give it about 4 to 24 hours to chill.

3. Once the chicken is ready, heat your grill up and grill every chicken for 5 to 6 minutes per side of the chicken. Ensure that the chicken is nicely cooked through with both sides having some grill marks. Remove them from the grill and place them on a tray to cool before cutting.

4. As the chicken cools, make the corn mixture by mixing all its ingredients in a medium-sized bowl then tossing them to ensure that they combine well. Set the dish aside.

5. Take the cool chicken pieces from the tray to a cutting board and dice it into cubes.

6. When assembling the burrito bowl, put a base of rice at the bottom of a bowl then add the toppings on it.

7. Serve with guacamole, if you desire.

Notes: I refrigerate my chicken for 24 hours so it can marinate nicely and get all the tasty flavors. It always turns out great. I am not sure if it will have the same kind of results if you refrigerate it for less than 24 hours.

For the burrito toppings, that I obviously omitted, you can use any that you like. You can use sour cream, cheese, tomatoes/salsa, beans, etc. These and many more will give you some yummy customized burrito dish of your own.

Alonti's Pecan Pesto Pasta

My husband's best friend and his wife love Alonti's. They have taken us there a few times, and I enjoyed the place. While there, I tried their Pecan Pesto, and I must admit that I enjoyed it a lot. It is my favorite dish at the restaurant so far.

Their pasta comes with grilled meat and some pesto, which is an amazing sauce. Pesto is a bit disadvantageous to make because you need pine nuts. However, Alonti's makes their pesto with pecans, thus making the sauce very unique.

Ingredients

½ cup Basil leaves

Extra virgin olive oil

Pecans to taste

2 Garlic cloves

Pinch Kosher salt

Parmesan cheese

Romano cheese

One package Cooked pasta

Instructions

1. Clean the basil leaves and put them in a food processor. Add some garlic and olive and pulse for a while until the garlic starts to break down into tiny pieces. Add the pecans and kosher salt and continue processing for a few more minutes at medium speed. Add the cheese and pulse until the cheese is uniformly mixed with the other ingredients.

2. When ready, pour the pesto on the cooked pasta and stir well.

Note: In case you do not plan on eating all the pesto at once, you can use an air-tight container to store the remaining pesto and keep it fresh for a few days.

Olive Garden Steak Gorgonzola Alfredo

I bet by now you have noticed that I love Olive Garden. I have gone there for lunch several times with friends, my husband, and sometimes my mom.

Another dish I find savory is the Steak Gorgonzola Alfredo. This is a recipe a lot of people want to know, so I decided to make a copycat dish of it and see how it turns out.

For those who love alfredo sauce and steak, this dish may turn out to be your favorite. The seared steak comes with the well-known alfredo sauce from Olive Garden; I do not see how you would not fall in love with this dish. I have included a bit of luscious gorgonzola cheese and a bit of fresh spinach.

Ingredients

Steak sirloin

Pepper and salt to taste (A lot to use for the Alfredo Sauce as well)

Vegetable oil

I package of Pasta

Butter

1 cup Heavy cream

Grated fresh Parmesan cheese

1 tsp Garlic powder

1/2 cup Tomatoes sundried in oil

1 package Fresh and clean baby spinach

Gorgonzola cheese

Balsamic Vinegar

Instructions

1. Take the steak and season it with pepper and salt. Put about 2 teaspoons of vegetable oil in a hot skillet. Once the oil is hot, place the steak in the skillet and cook until it is well-done to your desired taste. Set it aside and give it time to rest.

2. Prepare the pasta as per the directions on the package.

3. As for the Alfredo sauce, put the heavy cream and butter in a medium-sized pot. Heat the two on medium heat until they start producing some bubbles. Add the garlic powder and Parmesan cheese, then continuously stir until the cheese becomes molten. Simmer down the temperature, and give the sauce some time to cool.

4. When assembling, put the pasta on a plate, top up with the washed spinach, and toss. Pour in Alfredo sauce to pasta and spinach, then put them on a plate. Place pieces of the steak on the pasta and then add the

gorgonzola and cut sundried tomatoes toppings. Put the pasta and steak below the broiler until the cheese starts to turn brown.

Balsamic glaze:

In a small pot, pour the balsamic vinegar and heat over medium heat until half of the vinegar is gone.

Glaze the hot balsamic vinegar on the steak before you serve.

Chick fil A Mac and Cheese

Most people love mac and cheese, especially when home over the weekends, and just want to fix some quick lunch. Now, you may be wondering, is there a fast-food restaurant that makes delicious macaroni and cheese? Well, I can confidently attest to the fact that there is.

Many times, when you go out to a restaurant and eat mac and cheese, you will get dry and flavorless pasta. However, things are different at Chick fil A. They seem to naturally know the needs of their customers, thus making very delicious macaroni with creamy cheese. The cheese topping is even brown. If I were asked to choose the restaurant with the best mac and cheese, I would go for Chick fil A any time. Go there and give it a try, or better yet, you can try this recipe at home and bring Chick fil A mac and cheese home.

Ingredients

16 ounces macaroni

1 tablespoon salt

1 1/4 pounds American cheese

2 tablespoons Parmesan cheese

1 tablespoon Romano cheese

2 cups heavy cream

4 ounces Colby Jack Cheese shredded

Instructions

1. Put water in a large pot to about 2/3. Add a tablespoon of salt and boil. When the water is boiled, add pasta and let it cook to al dente. When ready, take the pot from the heater and drain the pasta.

2. Add the American cheese, heavy cream, Romano cheese, and Parmesan cheese in a medium-sized pot. Melt the heavy cream together with all the cheeses over medium heat. Keep stirring them from time to time to keep the cheese from scorching.

3. Turn on the oven to high for it to broil.

4. Put the cooked pasta in a baking dish then, over the pasta, pour in the cheeses that are now melted.

5. Top up the pasta with some shredded Colby Jack cheese then place the dish under the broiler.

6. Broil the dish until the cheese starts turning brown.

Red Lobster Lobster Pizza

You can find this original dish at Red Lobster. Just as the name suggests, Red Lobster Restaurant has got to have Lobster Pizza. I have tasted it once, and I immediately knew that I should try it at home.

It is very easy and quick to make for lunch when chilling with family at home over the weekend or on holidays.

Ingredients

½ pound Lobster meat, cut into chunks

Flour tortillas (one for every pizza)

Drained and diced Roma tomatoes (to taste)

1 cup or more Shredded Italian cheese blend

Grated fresh parmesan cheese to taste

Garlic butter - Roasted in oil

Fresh basil, cut into julienne strips

Instructions

1. Heat the oven to 450°F.

2. Brush the whole top of the tortilla lightly with the garlic butter. Ensure that you brush from one edge to another.

3. On the garlic butter, sprinkle about 2 tablespoons of Parmesan cheese.

4. Once you drain the diced tomatoes, evenly sprinkle them on the Parmesan cheese.

5. To cut the basil to julienne strips, clean it and shake to rid off the excess water. Pluck off the leaves and mound them on top of each other. Cut them into 1/8" strips using a chef's knife. Be sure not to chop them. When done, evenly sprinkle them on the diced tomatoes.

6. Cut the lobster meat into chunks, portion it, then drain. Sprinkle it evenly on the tomatoes.

7. On the diced tomatoes, evenly sprinkle the Italian six-cheese blend then place the dish in the fridge until when you are ready to cook it.

8. Lightly brush a pizza pan with vegetable oil then gently sprinkle the kosher salt and ground black

pepper on it. Do not forget this part as it is very important.

9. Once the oven is set, put the pizza on the baking pan, place it in the oven and let it bake for roughly 4 to 5 minutes.

10. Transfer from pan to a flat surface and divide it into several wedges.

11. For extra flavor, squeeze some fresh lemon on the pizza then serve.

Note: Ensure that you drain the lobster meat and tomatoes before you sprinkle them on the pizza crust. If not, your pizza will become soggy once it is cooked.

Bucca di Beppo's Three Meat Sauce

Bucca di Beppo is one of the restaurants whose pasta sauces I love. I think it is among the best I have tasted so far. They usually combine pepperoni, Italian sausage, and ground beef to create some meaty sauce that is excellent for any pasta dish. Try this, and I bet you will not be disappointed.

Ingredients

1 lbs. Ground beef

1 cup Finely chopped pepperoni

Large Jar of Marinara sauce

Olive oil

1 tbsp. Italian seasonings

1 can Crushed tomatoes

2 Uncased Italian sausages

½ cup Chopped onions

Instructions

1. In a large pot, sauté the onions in a little olive oil. Once the onions become frosted, add the chopped tomatoes and two jars of marina sauce. Turn down the heat to simmer.

2. Cook the Italian sausage ground beef in a large skillet until well-cooked. Drain the meat of the fat then add it to the sauce. To the mixture, add the chopped pepperoni and the Italian seasonings then simmer for around 30 minutes before adding pepper and salt to taste.

3. Serve with pasta.

Note: This dish can be so good for large families since it is possible to make a large pot of sauce. To add the amount of sauce, increase the amount of marinara and tomatoes. Before you make any adjustments, wait until all the meat is seasoned since there is a lot of different savory meats.

For smaller families, you can freeze any leftover sauce to use later.

DINNER RECIPES

Dinners are the most formal and meal of the day. Most people prefer to have it in the evening together with family. Well, people in history ate the largest meal at around midday. They used to call it dinner.

The elite in Western culture gradually changed the timing around the 16th to 19th centuries. Nonetheless, the word "dinner" stuck and has been used for different meanings in different cultures. Some eat it in the afternoon – early or late – or even on special occasions. For instance, usually, people observe a Christmas dinner. People in hot climates tend to take their main meal after the temperature falls in the evening.

No matter what time you eat it, dinner is a great meal to never miss and best shared with those you love.

Here are a few copycat recipes of the best dinners I have had in restaurants.

Panda Express Beijing Beef

So, I love me some Chinese food sometimes, and when I want to grab some, I always find myself at Panda Express. I guess their Beijing Beef is the reason I go there often. I find it very filling and sweet.

So, I tried a copycat recipe at home, which came out nice. It is pretty easy to make and takes less than an hour - probably 45 minutes or so.

Ingredients

Thin strips of flank steak

Cornstarch, for dusting

Frying oil

½ cup Water

1 Egg

2 tsp Cornstarch

Pinch of Salt

Pinch Crushed chili pepper

½ cup Ketchup

¼ cup Sugar

1 tbsp Vinegar

½ cup Water

½ cup Sliced white onion

1 tbsp Minced garlic

Diced green bell pepper

Diced red bell pepper

Instructions

1. Slice the beef into thin strips.

2. Combine all the ingredients of the marinade in a sealable bag and mix well. Add the slices of beef and give it about 15 minutes to marinate.

3. As the beef marinades, combine all the sauce ingredients in a bowl and put in the fridge to chill.

4. Once the beef is ready, use the cornstarch to marinate the slices of beef. Take off any excess cornstarch then put it in a wok or deep fryer to cook. You can cook slices of beef in batches. You will know they are cooked when they float and turn golden brown. When ready, place them on paper towels to drain.

5. Pour a little oil to the wok - about 2 tablespoons and add some minced garlic. Stir for about 15 seconds, then add the onions and red and green bell peppers. Continue stirring for a couple of minutes. Transfer the vegetables from the wok and set aside.

6. Take the wok again and pour in the sauce. Heat it until it boils.

7. When serving, put the vegetables and beef together in a serving pot and pour the sauce on it to coat.

San Jacinto Pork Carnitas

I have heard a lot of people talking about the Pork Carnitas at San Jacinto in my neighborhood. A lot of people are in love with it. I had to try it just to find out for myself - and yes, I understood what the buzz was all about. Slow-baked in the oven, these carnitas come out just fine.

So, maybe you have thought about ways to make it at home. Maybe you would want to serve it to your friends at the next potluck. Well, here is a copycat recipe for the pork carnitas that you can make at home.

Ingredients

Pork roast, about 2 pounds, but can be more or less

Juniper berries

Salt

Sunflower oil

Ground black pepper

½ cup Water

1 tsp. Thyme

Instructions

1. Preheat the oven to 350 degrees.

2. Add to a Dutch oven some sunflower oil and heat over medium heat.

3. Use the salt to season the roast. Once the oil is well-heated, sauté the roast for about 3 to 4 minutes on all sides. The roast will turn a bit brown. When ready, put the meat in a Dutch Oven and add bay leaves, ground black pepper, thyme, juniper berries, and water. Put it in the oven and give it about 3 to 4 hours to cook. Keep turning the roast over after every hour to ensure that the roast gets the maximum amount of flavors in it.

4. Take the roast from the oven and let it rest for about 15 minutes.

5. Place lid on the pan and cook for in the oven. Turn roast over in the pot every hour or so. Turning the roast will ensure the flavors go through the roast. Use a fork to pull the meat apart when serving.

6. Remove roast from the oven. Allow resting for about 20 minutes. Then pull the meat apart with two folks.

If you are using a slow cooker:

1. Put a large skillet on the kitchen stove and turn on the heat to medium. Add sunflower to it. As the oil becomes hot, season the roast with salt. Put the roast in the hot oil and sauté for about 4 minutes on every side.

2. Put the meat in a slow cooker then add some thyme, water, bay leaves, ground black pepper, and juniper berries. Cover with a lid and let it cook on medium heat for about 3 to 4 hours. Keep turning after every hour as it ensures the meat is fully flavored.

Note: I suggest that you do not use a pressure cooker for this recipe. There is a better flavor to the meat when it roasts slowly.

Be sure to pick a cut of pork that has marbling; you can always trim the fat after cooking.

You can skip out on the Juniper berries. However, that will change the flavor a bit.

If you would like Keto-friendly food, you can use avocado oil.

Romano's Macaroni Grill Chicken Rigatoni

Sometimes I like to spoil myself. Romano's Macaroni Grill is two blocks from my office. So, I went there one day with a friend. We had gone to discuss some business ideas that we had, but we did not really get to finish our discussion. Our talk was distracted by the taste of the Chicken Rigatoni that we were both eating for the first time.

A couple of weeks later, my friend sent me a text message and photos. She had made the chicken rigatoni at home. She could not wait to share the photos of her family enjoying the fruit of her efforts.

This dish is very easy to make. It takes about 35 to 40 minutes to prepare.

Ingredients

1-2 pounds of Grilled chicken

1 package Rigatoni pasta

2 tbsp Cooking wine

Butter-flavored oil

1 cup Mushrooms

Salt and pepper to taste

½ cup Caramelized onion

Parmesan cheese

Basil

½ cup Heavy cream

Instructions

1. Put the mushrooms, chicken, butter, salt and pepper, caramelized onions, basil, and flavored oil in a hot sauté and sauté for about 1 hour and 30 minutes.

2. After the 1 hr 30 minutes are done, add some wine to the mix and sauté for another few seconds. Add some heavy cream to it and let it boil over high heat.

3. Immerse the pre-cooked pasta in simmering water for a few then seconds then drain completely.

4. Pour the pasta in the sauté pan and cook until they mix well. Toss them a bit while still on the fire.

5. Add some parmesan cheese and keep tossing until the cheese is well-combined.

6. Put it on the plate and sprinkle some parsley for garnish.

Olive Garden Zuppa Toscana

If you have had the Zuppa Toscana Soup at Olive Garden, you may have wondered how the dish could be made at home. Well, I was so amazed by it, the foodie in me left that restaurant with a goal to make one just like it. Well, I tried, and I made it. I got to see that you can bring Olive Garden's Zuppa Toscana right to your home.

With some Italian sausage, onions, potatoes, cream, kale, and bacon, you can make your family some delicious soup filled with a mother's love.

Ingredients

Hot or sweet Italian sausage links – at least two

½ cup Heavy cream

Minced garlic

Peeled and halved russet potatoes- at least 2 depending on the size

Salt and pepper

1 small Chopped onion

2 cup Water

4 cups Chicken broth

Real Bacon Bits

2 cups Chopped kale

Instructions

1. Preheat the oven to 350 degrees F.

2. In a baking pan, place the sausages and for about 30 minutes, roast until they are well-cooked through. When ready, drain them on paper towels and use a knife to slice them.

3. Put the potatoes, garlic, onions, water, and chicken broth in a pot and cook until potatoes are done on medium heat. When they are ready, add the bacon, sausage, pepper, and salt to taste then simmer for an extra 10 minutes. Simmer down the heat. After the 10 minutes, put in the kales, cream, and some more water, if needed. Cook it thoroughly then serve.

Cajun Café Bourbon Chicken

When you go to shopping malls, you will often find bourbon chicken. Well, Cajun Cafe did a twist of that bourbon chicken and made an even better version of it.

It is so nice and easy to make. You can use all parts of a chicken from the thighs, the legs, and the chicken breasts.

Ingredients

Chunks of chicken thigh or leg meat

½ cup Bourbon Whiskey

1 tbsp Soy sauce

1 tbsp White wine

1 tsp Corn starch

2 tbsp Brown sugar

1 tsp Powdered ginger

1 tsp Garlic powder

Water

1 tbsp Dried minced onion

Instructions

1. Put the chicken in a bowl. Mix all the ingredients of the marinade and pour them on the pieces of chicken. Cover the bowl and put the chicken in the fridge to chill. Keep it for several hours, occasionally stirring it to ensure it is well-flavored. It is best if you let it chill overnight.

2. When properly chilled, bake the chicken for an hour at 350 in a single layer. Baste it after every 10 to 15 minutes.

3. Remove the chicken from the marinade, shake off the extra pan juices then place them on a frying pan. Heat it and pour in a little white wine.

4. For the corn starch slurry, combine the corn starch with water and mix it well.

5. Pour in the corn starch slurry in the pan chicken juices and stir until the sauce becomes thick.

6. When properly thick, add in the chicken and let it cook for an extra minute.

Jay's Oyster House Baked Parmesan Shrimp

One of the most popular dishes at a restaurant I ate at while traveling is the Baked Parmesan Shrimp at Jay's Oyster House in Louisiana. They usually combine shrimp, some creamy parmesan sauce, fresh chopped tomatoes, and breadcrumbs to make this wonderful dish. Light and easy to make, this shrimp recipe is just what you need when you want something light for dinner in the evening.

Ingredients

1 package of Pasta

Peeled, deveined and cooked shrimp

Butter

½ cup Parmesan cheese

½ cup Heavy cream

Chopped parsley chopped

Melted butter

Diced Roma tomato

½ cup Breadcrumbs

Instructions

1. Preheat the oven to about 350 degrees.

2. Combine the heavy cream and butter in a medium-size saucepan. Heat it until the butter melts completely, and the batter gets to a simmer. Add into the pot, some Parmesan cheese, and stir until it melts. Season with white pepper, if you wish, and salt.

3. In a bowl, pour in the cooked pasta, then stir in the sauce and mix to evenly coat the pasta. Transfer the pasta to a couple of little casserole dishes.

4. In a bowl, combine the bread crumbs, Parmesan cheese, and melted butter. Stir to coat the cheese and butter well on the bread crumbs. (Optional step)

5. Sprinkle the bread crumbs into the casserole dish then place a few shrimp pieces into the casserole. Place it in the oven and bake until they are all well-heated through.

6. Used parsley and chopped tomatoes to garnish, if you like.

SIDE DISHES

Sometimes when you go to a restaurant or an event, you will be served a dish on the side of the main dish. Well, that dish is known as the side dish. It is simply an accompaniment to the main course and is usually smaller than the main course.

The side dish's purpose is to bring balance to the main dish and compliment it. It could have some mellowing flavor in some cases and, in others, a bit of spice. They can be used together with the main dish. For instance, it can be a sauce that you soak some bits of the main dish or a foundation for the main dish to sit.

Cracker Barrel Sprouts and Kale Salad

If you love greens and would like to enjoy some Brussels sprouts and some leafy green kale, I would recommend going to Cracker Barrel. They have some salad made of kales and sprouts that is to die for. This Sprouts and Kale salad is similar to coleslaw but flavored with crunchy pecans, craisins, and a maple dressing. If you love green and healthy veggies, try this dish. It may end up being your favorite as there is none like it.

Ingredients

1 cup Finely sliced kale

1 cup Chopped Brussel sprouts

1 tbsp White vinegar

3 tsp Maple syrup (Note: not the pancake syrup)

Pecans to taste

Craisins to taste

Vegetable oil

1 tbsp Dijon mustard

1 tsp Sugar

Salt

Instructions

1. Clean the kale with clean water and dry them.

2. Chop off the stems from every kale stalk as they can be tough ad woody.

3. Roll up the leaves to the shape similar to a cigar then slice them into fine slices. If the kale slices are long, cut them horizontally to break them up into small pieces.

4. Clean the sprouts with water and dry. Chop off the end of the stem and cut the Brussel sprouts into two. Place the sprout's cut flat side on the chopping board and cut them into small pieces.

5. Add the sliced Brussel sprouts, cut kales, pecans, and craisins in a bowl.

6. Put the maple syrup, white vinegar, salt, vegetable oil, Dijon mustard, and sugar in a small bowl and thoroughly whisk until it is well-blended.

7. Pour the well-combined dressing on the vegetables, and mix well. Cover the bowl with the salad with a lid and place in the fridge to chill for at least 30 minutes before you serve it.

KFC Coleslaw

Almost everyone has had this salad at KFC. They pair it with their pulled pork as well as their fried chicken. So sweet and tangy, this salad's copycat recipe will give you the more of the same kind of coleslaw you enjoy at KFC.

This recipe is easy to make and takes less than an hour to fix.

Ingredients

1 head of Cabbage

Half chopped onion

2 teaspoons Aragon vinegar

1/2 cup of sugar

3 teaspoons vegetable oil

2 Miracle Whip

2 carrots

Instructions

1. Mix the sugar, onions, and oil in a bowl.

2. Add the tarragon vinegar and mix in the Miracle Whip

3. Pour in the cabbage and grated carrots and mix them well.

4. In an air-tight dish, put in the mixture and place in the fridge to chill for a while. Preferably, the whole night before you serve it.

Note: The secret ingredient is the tarragon vinegar.

KFC Potato Wedges

KFC always has something that most people love. Many, including me, have gone to KFC for a quick snack. I have tried their potato wedges, and they are great for a quick french-fried pick-me-up. I would recommend that you make these sometime when you have guests over or the next potluck in your neighborhood.

Ingredients

4 pounds Russet potatoes

2 egg

1 teaspoon onion powder

2 teaspoons poultry seasoning optional

2 teaspoon garlic salt

3 cups flour

2 teaspoons salt

2 tablespoons ground black pepper

2 cup milk

Frying oil

Instructions

1. Combine the eggs and milk in a bowl and whisk thoroughly.

2. Add flour, black pepper, salt, poultry seasoning, onion powder, and garlic salt in another bowl and mix.

3. Clean the potatoes properly, then chop them into small wedges. Try your best to make them as uniform as possible.

4. For the potato preparation, dip the potatoes in the flour and coat, soak in the egg wash then dredge them once again with the flour. Set potatoes on a wire rack above a baking sheet and give them about 5 minutes to dry. When you give the potatoes time to dry, the coating on them will firm up and stick on the potatoes better.

5. Heat the oil to 350 degrees and fry the potatoes for about 6 to 7 minutes. When ready, place them on a wire rack for the oil to drain. This is the first round of cooking.

6. When the first round is done, place the potatoes in batches back into the oil to fry for an extra 4 minutes. When you fry them for the second time, the outer coating of the potatoes will become very crisp. Remove them from the oil to the wire rack to drain for the second time. When all of them are done, serve immediately when still hot.

Lee's Famous Recipe Corn on the Cob

I once went to Ohio to pay my aunt a visit. While I was there for the weekend, I popped in at Lee's Famous Recipe Chicken. I had a really great lunch at that place. What especially stood out to me was their corn on the cob side dish. It was so wonderfully spiced. I tried my best to feel all the ingredients in the cob, so I would make it at home for my husband, who is a big fan of corn. I bought a few to take to my aunt for her to have a taste of the goodness in her city.

This recipe is very simple. It will not even take you more than 15 minutes to fix.

Ingredients

6 Ears of corn

2 tbsp Old Bay Seasoning

6 tbsp Butter

Instructions

1. Boil water on high in a pot over a stove.

2. Shuck the corn, ensuring that you remove all the silks from them.

3. Put the corn in the boiling water and let it cook for 6 to 8 minutes.

4. Melt the butter as the corn cooks.

5. Once the corn is ready, take it out of the hot water, glaze it with the melted butter, then sprinkle the Old Bay Seasoning on them.

Note: You can use other kinds of seasoning salt to season the corn. I sometimes use Cajun spice blends, jalapeno salt, and barbecue rub to season the corn. I love them because they add some really nice flavor to the corn. So feel free to use the seasonings you love for this one.

Dickey's Barbecue Baked Potato Casserole

I know Dickey's Barbecue Pit is known for some really delicious barbecue. However, they also have some really yummy side dishes that complement their barbecue really well. One of those side dishes is Dickey's Baked Potato Casserole, which I must admit, you will love when you get to try it. Or better yet when you make it at home.

Ingredients

6 Russet potatoes

1/2 cup butter

2 teaspoon salt

1/2 cup sliced tops of green onion

1 cup sour cream

3/4 teaspoon ground black pepper

1 cup milk

1 cup shredded Cheddar cheese

Instructions

1. Preheat the oven to 425 degrees.

2. Clean the potatoes well and put them in the oven to bake for an hour. Do not poke holes into the potatoes as doing so will make the potatoes less light and fluffy. Also, keep checking up on the potatoes to keep them from being overcooked, which may make the potatoes explode inside the oven.

3. When ready and cool enough, place the white flesh in a bowl and mash until it is nicely smooth. Add in the sour cream, milk, butter, pepper, salt, and bits of bacon.

4. Spray a casserole dish with cooking spray and spoon in the potatoes. use the green onion tops, shredded cheese, and remaining bits of bacon to garnish. Place the dish in the oven and bake for 350 degrees. give it about 15 minutes to cook until the cheese starts melting.

Boston Market Creamed Spinach

I have gone to Boston Market about twice in my life. While there, I loved their Creamed Spinach. It is not only savory but also wonderfully creamy, making one want to go back there several times. This dish might be the lucky pot to win over your kids to spinach. I know several people who do not like spinach for some reason, but this Boston Market creamy spinach may make them change their minds.

Ingredients

1 package Chopped spinach

1 small Chopped onion

½ cup Water

Salt

1 cup Sour Cream

1 cup Whole Milk

Butter

Salt

2 tbsp Flour

Instructions

1. With a setting that is medium-low, make the white sauce by melting the butter in a pot then adding flour and some salt until it is nicely creamy.

2. On medium heat, pour in a little milk at a time. Keep stirring with a whisk from time to time until the mixture is smooth and thick. Pour the butter in a saucepan, add onions and cook on medium heat. Cook them until the onions become clear.

3. Put the spinach in and top with water. Simmer down the heat, cover the pan and give it time to cook. Occasionally stir until the spinach is nearly cooked completely. Sprinkle in a little salt and give it 2 seconds to cook. When the spinach is nearly cooked, add the sour cream and white sauce, mix properly, then simmer until it blends well.

Note: To make the spinach creamier, add to the sauce a few tablespoons of cream cheese.

When using frozen spinach, use paper towels to better squeeze out the extra water.

Wendy's Fondue Fries

This is inspired by the side dish I had at Wendy's. Have you tried these Fondue Fries? If not, you are missing out on some palatal heaven.

These French fries are coated with some cheese fondue sauce prepared with smoked bacon and Gruyere cheese.

Ingredients

30 ounces frozen French fries

2 tablespoon butter

1 cup shredded Gruyere cheese

2 tablespoon flour

1 cup of milk

6 pieces applewood cooked smoked bacon

1/4 teaspoon salt

Instructions

1. Melt the butter in a saucepan over medium heat. Once it melts, add the flour to the butter. Mix the flour nicely and take about 1 minute to cook until the flour starts to produce some cooked pie crust-like fragrance.

2. Add some salt to simmer then half of the milk in and stir. Ensure you stir well until the mixture is well-thick. When properly thick, pour in the rest of the milk and stir until it is thick again. Put in the shredded cheese and stir until all the cheese is melted.

3. Preheat the oil to about 350 degrees then fry the French fries until their color turns to a golden brown. When ready, take them out of the oil and place them on a wire rack to drain.

4. When serving, place the French fries on a platter, top up with the fondue cheese sauce, then finish with the bits of cooked bacon.

DESSERT RECIPES

As the last dish in a meal, dessert is usually sweet. A favorite to those with a sweet tooth.

A meal in a big family is not whole without some sweet homemade dessert. I have gone out a lot for dinners at several restaurants and sampled a number of desserts. Some really stuck out to me, and I came up with copycat recipes for them. I hope you find your favorite among these. Most of them are simple when it comes to preparation and will be yummy and great for you and your family or friends.

Taco Bell Cinnamon Twists

There was a time I just could not get enough of the cinnamon twists at Taco Bell. So, I decided to make my own to enjoy in the comfort of my home. This recipe turned out just as crunchy and sweet as the real Taco Bell cinnamon twists.

Ingredients

7 ounces spiral-shaped Duros

Frying oil

7 tablespoon cinnamon

1 cup of sugar

Instructions

1. Mix the sugar, cinnamon, and spiral-shaped Duros in a dish and stir.

2. Heat the frying oil until it is 350 degrees hot.

Put several pieces of the Duros in the oil at once, and cook. After a few minutes, you will see the Duros puff up. Once they get puffy, let them cook for an extra 5 seconds. Remove from the oil.

Shoney's Hot Fudge Cake

My friend had gone to Shoney's with another friend of hers a couple of years ago. She enjoyed the meals that she had there but kept talking about one - the hot fudge cake. This dessert is so yummy with ice cream sandwiched in the middle of devil food cake. Though we see less of Shoney's than before, their dessert is still epic and can be made easily at home.

Ingredients

Devil's Food Cake Mix(Duncan Hines)

1 tsp Vanilla extract or paste

2 Eggs

½ cup Cold water

¼ cup Chocolate syrup

1 scoop Vanilla bean ice cream

Vegetable oil

Kosher salt

Fudge Sauce

Chopped bittersweet chocolate

1 can Condensed milk(Sweetened)

½ cup Corn syrup (Regular or dark)

Dry cherries

Water

Vanilla extract or paste

Heavy pinch salt

Canned whipped cream or homemade mildly sweetened whipped cream

Instructions

1. Prepare the oven for the Cake by heating it to 350F.

2. Lightly brush some oil in a metal cake pan and set aside. In a large bowl, put the cake mix plus the other cake ingredients and mix using a hand mixer. Do this for about 30 seconds on low speed. Rub the bowl then mix on medium speed for an extra couple of minutes. Scrape off the bowl as required.

3. Pour and smoothen out the batter into the ready pan. Put it an oven and bake for 25-30 minutes. To know if the cake is ready, press it lightly and observe to see if it springs back up. If it does, then the cake is ready. When ready, transfer it from the cake pan to a rack and let it cool for about 15 minutes.

4. Turn the cake on the cooling rack, strip the parchment off and give the cake more time to cool completely.

5. For the Fudge Sauce, put all the ingredients apart from the vanilla in a saucepan whose bottom is heavy. Heat them on medium heat and constantly stir until all of the chocolate is melted. Transfer the pan from the stove to another surface and add in the vanilla. When you put the vanilla after removing the pan from the stove, it will ensure that it does not evaporate. Keep the sauce warm. In case it cools down, re-heat it before you serve.

6. When assembling, smoothen the cake's top with a knife if need be. This will ensure that the pieces of cake are equally thick and uniform when you serve them. Carefully slice the cake horizontally, leaving the halves in place. Every half can be approximately 3/4 inch in thickness.

7. Set half a share of the cake aside, then spread two long, extended plastic wrap sheets on the counter and put the rectangular base part of the cake on the wrap. Strip off the cardboard from around the ice cream.

8. Slice and arrange the ice cream into 3/4" slices. Touch them nicely on top of the layer of cake. To fit well, you will have to scrape off some of it. Place the other rectangular part of the cake atop the ice cream and lightly press down. In the plastic wrap, wrap the cake and put it in a freezer for about 2 to 3 hours to freeze.

9. Serve the slices of cake into squares and drench them with some fudge sauce on top. Add some whipped cream and a cherry as toppings.

Cracker Barrel Coke Cake

Cracker Barrel restaurants have some great desserts. I have had some of their Coke cake and, I must say, it is very sweet and tasty.

To prepare this cake, you need about an hour. With this recipe, you will have a yummy cake that is almost similar to the Coke cake at Cracker Barrel.

Ingredients

4 cups unbleached all-purpose flour

2 cup Coca Cola

4 cups of sugar

4 eggs

7 tablespoons unsweetened cocoa powder

2 teaspoon vanilla

2 cup unsalted butter 2 sticks

1 cup buttermilk

2 teaspoon baking soda

5 tablespoons unsweetened cocoa powder

6 cups confectioners' sugar

10 ounces marshmallow cream

10 tablespoons Coca Cola

1 cup unsalted butter

2 teaspoon vanilla

Instructions

1. Preheat the oven to 350°F. With a with nonstick spray, spray the baking pan.

2. Combine the flour, baking soda, and granulated sugar in a bowl and mix. When ready, set it aside.

3. Melt the butter in a small saucepan together with the Coca Cola and cocoa. Whisk together as it boils to high.

4. When ready, pour the tepid chocolate batter on the flour mixture and thoroughly mix until well-

combined. Combine the mixture with vanilla, eggs, and buttermilk. Keep whisking until it is well-combined. When ready, pour the mixture in the prepared baking pan and place it in the oven to bake for about 45 minutes.

5. In the last 15 minutes of baking, start preparing the frosting.

6. Place the marshmallow cream aside and, in a large mixing bowl, sift the confectioners' sugar. Melt the butter, Coca Cola, and cocoa powder and whisk well until the mixture boils. Take it from heat, put some vanilla and mix.

7. On the sifted confectioners' sugar, pour the tepid chocolate mixture and whisk continuously until it is thoroughly combined.

8. Take the cake out of the oven and quickly leak some drops of marshmallow cream atop the hot cake. Give it about a minute or so to rest.

9. Spread the marshmallow cream carefully on the cake then slowly drop the warm chocolate coating over the layer of marshmallow.

Reese's Peanut Butter Eggs

Reese's have been so good at giving us the best Peanut Butter Eggs, especially during Easter. When I was a kid, my mother would always have a few of these in the Easter basket. She taught us that an Easter basket is not complete until a few peanut butter eggs are in it.

Well, good news, you can bring Reese's home with a few peanut butter eggs of your own. This yummy dessert is not only delicious but also easy to make.

Ingredients

2 cups of peanut butter

32 ounces chocolate

2 cup powdered sugar

2 teaspoon vanilla

1/2 cup butter

4 tablespoons butter

Instructions

1. Combine butter and peanut butter together in a medium-sized bowl and use a mixer to blend. Add the vanilla and powdered sugar and mix for a couple of minutes.

2. To shape the eggs, scoop the peanut butter batter using a teaspoon and shape it with your hands until it is egg-shaped. Put the eggs on a wax paper-lined cookie sheet and place them in the fridge to cool. Give them about 30 minutes before you coat them with the chocolate.

3. As the eggs cool, melt the chocolate in a microwave or double boiler for around 30 to 45 seconds. Put a little butter in the chocolate then mix to combine them well. Once the chocolate-butter mix is well-molten, set it aside.

4. Take the peanut butter eggs from the fridge and lightly dip every one of them into the chocolate-butter mix. Set the chocolate-drenched eggs on the waxed paper. Give the chocolate some time to set. When the chocolate is nicely firm, serve the eggs and enjoy.

Note: You can use coconut oil as an alternative to the butter if you desire.

Applebee's Blond Brownies

My brother and I loved going to Applebee's. We kept meeting there at least once a month like a tradition until he and his wife started an RV trip that has lasted for quite a while. So, one time, I had the Applebee's maple blondie.

For years, I have always thought of trying it out but always been caught up by other recipes and work stuff. I, however, finally got the opportunity to make it, and it turned out so yummy. Thanks to Applebee's, my dinner table has a new dessert that the kids love.

Ingredients

1 cup softened butter

1-3/4 cups chopped pecans

3 cups packed brown sugar

3 cups all-purpose flour

5 large eggs, room temperature

3 teaspoons vanilla extract

3 teaspoon salt

3 teaspoons baking powder

Chopped pecans and vanilla ice cream

2 cup maple syrup

1/2 cup evaporated milk

4 tablespoons butter

Instructions

1. Mix the butter and brown sugar in a large bowl until it is fluffy and light. Whisk in the vanilla and eggs and set aside.

2. Slowly combine the flour, salt, and baking powder then add the batter to the cream mixture. Mix in the pecans.

3. Lightly grease a baking dish then pour the mixture into it. Place it in the oven to bake for 25-30 minutes at 350°. Insert a toothpick at the center of the cake; if it comes out clean, then the cake is well-cooked. Transfer it from the oven to a wire rack to cool.

4. In a saucepan, combine the butter and the syrup to make the sauce. Put the mixture on a stove and bring

to a boil. Stir as it cooks for about 3 minutes. Transfer the mixture from the heat, then add some milk to it.

5. Divide the brownies into half or little squares if you like.

6. Set them on a dessert plate then place a scoop of ice cream on them. Finish with the sauce topping and a sprinkle of pecans.

Zapato's Barbecue Banana Pudding

The Banana Pudding at Zapato's Barbecue in Arizona reminded me of my mother. She loved making creamy vanilla pudding with crunchy Nilla wafers and fresh bananas. The thought of it just makes me homesick.

I got to try it at home, and here is the recipe I came up with.

Ingredients

1/2 cup all-purpose flour

1 cup of sugar

4 tablespoons butter

3 teaspoons vanilla

5 beaten egg yolks

3 ounces cream cheese

4 cups whole milk

50 Nilla wafers

3 large bananas

2 teaspoon sugar

2 cup heavy whipped cream

Instructions

1. Combine the milk, sugar, and flour in a heavy saucepan. Cook the mixture, continually stir on medium heat until the batter starts to bubble and become thick. Stir and cook it for an extra couple of minutes then transfer from the heat.

2. In a small bowl, place for egg yolks then beat them well. Slowly pour in a cup of the cooked pudding mixture in the beaten eggs, then stir the egg plus the pudding mixture well.

3. Slowly pour the whole mixture back into the pan, where the rest of the pudding mixture is. Heat the mixture until it begins to bubble. Combine some cream cheese, vanilla, and butter and stir the ingredients until they are well-combined.

4. Empty the pudding from the pan into a bowl then cover the surface with a plastic wrap. Put the pudding in the fridge to cool.

5. In a bowl, put in the heavy whipping cream and a teaspoon of sugar.

6. Whisk using a mixer until it stiffens. Put it in the fridge to cool for about 10 minutes before using it.

7. When assembling the pudding, break the vanilla wafers into every jar then slice the bananas into small slices. Place several banana slices on every jar then top up the bananas with a bit of pudding. pour the whipped cream on the pudding to finish. Do the same for every jar.

Note: The reason why a plastic wrap is used to cover the pudding as it cools is to prevent the top of the pudding from forming a skin.

You can use shortbread cookies in place of the vanilla wafers. For instance, you can go for Lorna Dune cookies.

DRINK RECIPES

Sometimes, I like making fancy drinks at home for my family or when some of our friends come over. I like to try different kinds of drink recipes that I have had in restaurants and some that I find online from coffee, shakes, smoothies, to cocktails.

With these recipes, you can have a fancy drink at the comfort of your home. You do not need to go out. Here, I have given you my favorite drinks from different restaurants

McDonald's Thin Mint Milkshake

If you have had the Shamrock Shake at McDonald's, then you would be familiar with this drink. Inspired by the Shamrock Shake, this creamy shake needs just a few cookies that both kids and adults enjoy. It is very simple and takes less than 10 minutes.

Ingredients

5 tablespoons of 2% milk with a bit of peppermint extract or 5 tablespoons creme de menthe

8 Girl Scout's Thin Mint cookies

2 cups vanilla ice cream

Food coloring, Green (Optional)

Instructions

Put all the ingredients in a blender, cover then blend until well-combined. Pour into glasses and serve immediately.

Red Robin Screaming Red Zombie

This drink from Red Robin is usually so strong, a drop of it may wake the dead. However, it is a great drink for the summer and a great drink to cool off.

Ingredients

1 cup Orange juice

1 tbsp Lemon juice

2 oz Bacardi Select Rum

1 oz Myer's Dark Rum

Sugar for the rim to garnish

1 oz Light Rum

Splash of Grenadine

Instructions

1. In a bowl, combine the lemon juice and sugar the mix until well-combined. Add in some rum and orange juice to the sweetened lemon juice and stir well.

2. Load some ice into a cup and pour the mixture on top of it. Float in the Myer's Dark Rum, Bacardi Select Rum, and Grenadine using a spoon in that order. For proper floating, use the back of the spoon to slowly pour in the ingredients mentioned in the drink. This is to ensure that they do not mix too much into the drink.

Starbucks Hibiscus Refresher

When going about my schedule in the city, I sometimes like to pop in at Starbucks to take a break from the day's hustle and bustle. This drink, based on tea, is cool for the afternoon and easy to make.

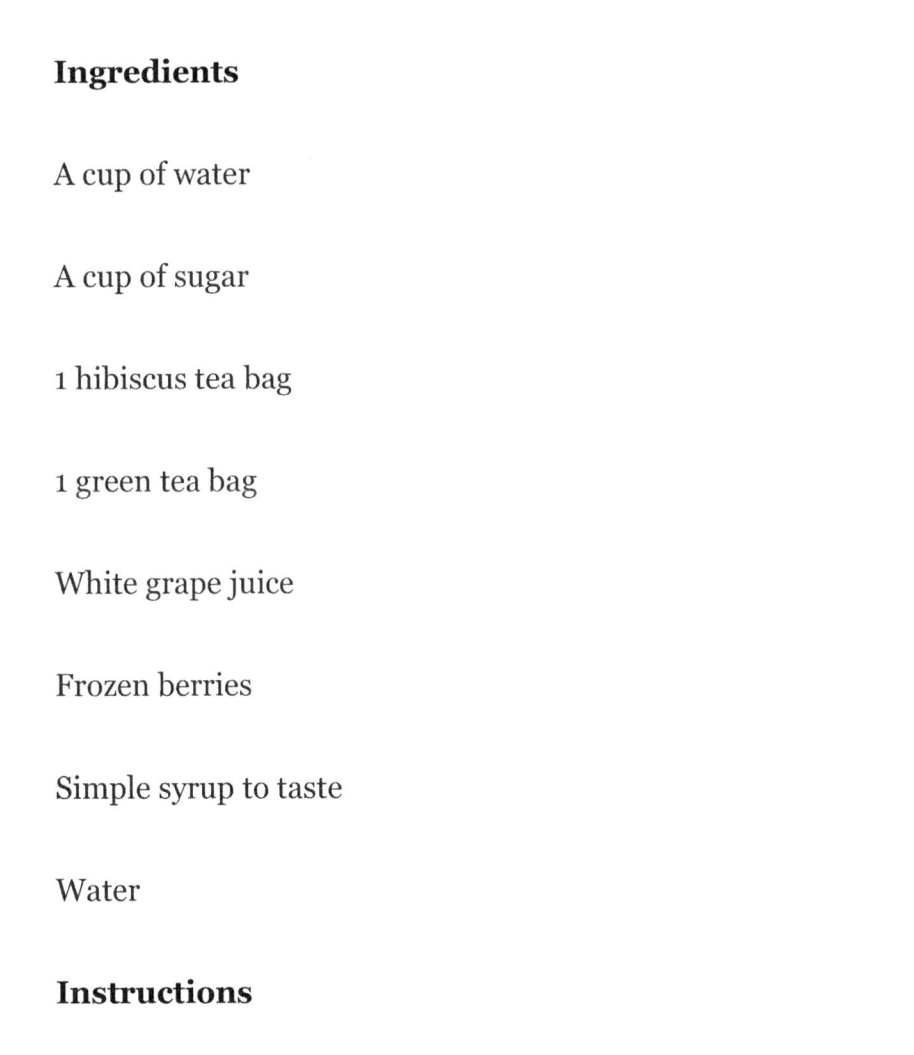

Ingredients

A cup of water

A cup of sugar

1 hibiscus tea bag

1 green tea bag

White grape juice

Frozen berries

Simple syrup to taste

Water

Instructions

1. Combine the sugar and water in a saucepan and mix thoroughly to make the simple syrup. Boil for a couple of minutes until the sugar is well dissolved into the water. Transfer from the heat and set aside for a couple of minutes to cool before you use it.

2. In two cups of water, brew the hibiscus and green, let it steep, then give it about 5 minutes to cool. Pour into a glass, the cooled tea, white grape juice, and cooled simple syrup, and stir to mix it well. Place some ice and frozen berries as toppings.

Dunkin Donuts Caramel Hot Chocolate

This drink at Dunkin Donuts is awesome at any time of the year. The good thing is you can also try it at home.

Ingredients

1/2 cup cocoa powder

3 tablespoons caramel syrup

1/2 cup sugar

2 tablespoons of salted caramel syrup

1/2 cup water

3 tablespoons whipped cream

1 cup milk

Instructions

1. Combine the sugar, cocoa powder, and water in a small saucepan, place it on a stove and boil. Ensure that you press any lumps that form. Simmer for a couple of minutes until the mix is warm and smooth. Add the milk into the mixture and heat.

2. Put the salted caramel syrup in a glass then pour in the hot chocolate. Top with the whipped cream, caramel sauce, and salt. Let it cool for a few minutes then serve.

Note: If you wish to use a microwave to make it, combine sugar and the cocoa powder in a glass. Heat the water and milk for a couple of minutes in the microwave then pour the mixture on the cocoa powder. To the same glass, put the salted caramel syrup and add the toppings as instructed above in the instructions above. Let it cool for a few minutes, serve, and enjoy.

Taco Bell Baja Blast Freeze

Awesome for a warm day, the Baja Blast Freeze from Taco Bell is a pleasant drink to make at home. Its recipe is very simple and takes a very short time.

Ingredients

10 ounces Mountain Dew

8 ounces ice

5 ounces Powerade Berry Blast

Instructions

Put all the ingredients in a mixer and blend well until the ice is totally crushed. Serve immediately.

Chili's Green Apple Sangria

One of my favorite drinks at Chili's is their Green Apple Sangria. It is so great for the falls. Prepared with Moscato wine, this drink is delicious and very easy to make.

Ingredients

850 mls Moscato

10 cups ice

8 ounces pineapple juice

1 cup orange slices

8 ounces Apple Pucker or Apple Puree (Granny Smith)

1 cup strawberries

1 cup green apple slices

Instructions

1. Combine the pineapple juice, granny smith apple puree, and chilled Moscato in a large pitcher and combine well.

2. In a glass, place some ice cubes then pour in the refreshment over the ice.

3. Serve immediately.

Copycat Cooking and Health

I hope by now, you are getting ready to go on this kitchen adventure with all these recipes. The sweetness in these meals will make you try them over and over again. You will never run out of options when deciding on what to make for dinner, lunch, or even breakfast.

Now, I am aware that a lot of people, including me, are keen on health matters. While most of the ingredients are healthy and delicious, some can be a bit unhealthy if consumed in large amounts or often.

We should observe our food intake and avoid foods that may bring health complications. Also, there are people who are allergic to different kinds of dishes. For this reason, it is good to be sensitive and make foods that will be suitable for them. These will require substitutes with allergen-friendly foods.

Well, fixing up a healthy meal is not as hard as it may seem. In fact, with a bit of adjustment to the recipes, you may be able to make the healthiest dishes for you and your family or friends.

Below is a simple guide to ingredient substitution that may help you get better alternatives to the ingredients in these recipes and many others that you may come across.

Healthy Substitutes

- Substitute dry bread crumbs with crushed bran cereal or rolled oats.

- Replace oil, margarine, butter, and shortening in baked products with prune puree or Applesauce for half of the butter, shortenings expressed for baking, or trans-fat free spreads.

- Use cooking spray to prevent sticking rather than butter, shortening, or margarine.

- Replace canned vegetables, meat, fish, and soups with reduced-sodium or low-sodium types.

- Instead of using cream, use evaporated skim milk or fat-free half-and-half.

- Use pureed low-fat cottage cheese, Neufchatel cheese, or low-fat/fat-free cream cheese in place of full-fat cream cheese.

- Use two egg whites for every whole egg as substitutes for eggs.

- Mix in half of the whole-wheat flour with half of the plain all-purpose flour required in a baking recipe.

- Replace ground beef with ground chicken breast, lean ground or extra-lean beef, or ground turkey breast.

- Do reduced-fat or reduced-calorie mayonnaise instead of mayonnaise.

- In soups, stews, and casseroles, use vegetables for half the meat required in the recipe.

- Use evaporated skim milk rather than evaporated milk and fat-free or reduced-fat milk rather than whole milk.

- Make the whole-wheat pasta instead of the enriched white pasta.

- Replace white rice with wild rice, pearl barley, brown rice, or bulgur wheat.

- For seasoning, replace onion salt, celery salt, or garlic salt with onion flakes, celery seed, or garlic powder. You can also do herb-based seasonings like chopped fresh garlic, onions, or celery.

- Use low-fat or fat-free sour cream, low-fat or plain fat-free yogurt in place of full-fat sour cream.

Allergen-friendly Foods

There are many people dealing with different kinds of allergies. There are specific foods that they can never ingest due to the allergens that they normally react negatively to. Some of these allergies include meat, soy, gluten, milk, and many others. For this reason, we must be very considerate of such people and make foods that they can enjoy without suffering any complications.

There are substitutes for some of these ingredients that people may be allergic to. They may not be similar in taste to the actual ingredients; however, they provide better and healthier options to the actual ingredients.

In case you are allergic or know someone who is allergic to some of the actual ingredients, give these substitutes a try and see how they turn out. You can also use them freely, even if you are not allergic to the actual products. They are much healthier as much as they may taste different.

Butter

Most dairy-free butter alternatives are margarine but beware since not all margarine is dairy-free. Many kinds of margarine are made from dairy derivatives like calcium caseinate, so do read labels carefully.

Brand names that are dairy-free include Earth Balance and Fleischmann's unsalted (note that Fleischmann's salted margarine contains whey). While most margarine contains trans fats, these also are trans-fat free. You'll find that margarine varies greatly in different brands' suitability for baking, but virtually all are fine for table use. If you need a dairy-free, soy-free alternative for baking, consider Spectrum Organics' Palm Oil Shortening.

Eggs

When baking, you can replace the eggs with a couple of great egg substitutes currently on the market. These are Bob's Red Mill Egg Replacer and Ener-G's Egg Replacer, which both hold leavening ingredients designed to simulate the role of eggs in baked products.

However, it is good to note that egg substitutes cannot be used in the case of an omelet, scrambled eggs, or even sauces that require eggs to thicken, such as Hollandaise.

Milk

In most supermarkets, you will find a wide variety of non-dairy milk substitutes. They are perfect for people who lactose intolerant or allergic to milk. Such people always react negatively to milk anytime they consume it through cooking, pouring over cereal, or even drinking. There is such a wide variety that you can find alternatives that have a mild taste and some with a lot of proteins. It all depends on the kind that you would prefer.

Ice Cream

In this category, you will find two kinds of alternatives. Some imitate the texture of ice cream while others are naturally dairy-free. Among the naturally dairy-free chilled dessert alternatives are fruit sorbets, frozen ices, and granitas. You should, however, check the labels when purchasing to make sure that there are no little added amounts of milk protein. These desserts are normally very sweet and mostly made from fruit.

Brands selling these dairy-free ice creams include Tofutti and So Delicious. You can find them in some large supermarkets as well as specialty groceries. Though they are closer to ice cream in texture, these substitutes are made from soy, which is also an allergen and stronger in taste than milk.

Mayonnaise

Maybe you do not want to consume the eggs in mayonnaise. Well, in such a case, you can buy the veganaise, which is the vegan mayonnaise. You can also make your own and avoid the soy, sulfites, and corn in the mayonnaise. You can make mayonnaise easily. However, it traditionally requires raw eggs.

Soy Sauce

For those allergic to soy, it is best to know that there is currently no alternative product in the market that substitutes soy sauce as well. It is challenging to find soy sauce substitutes as a seasoning or for dips. Nevertheless, you may enjoy the Thai fermented fish in some food recipes. The Thai fermented fish is nearly ever produced without soy.

To replace the wheat in soy sauce brewed traditionally, use tamari soy sauce, which is produced without wheat. The most available brand in this category is the San-J and Bragg's Liquid Aminos, whose soy sauce is gluten-free and wheat-free, respectively.

Cream

You can use soy powder-thickened soy milk, melted margarine, soy coffee cream, or coconut milk as a substitute for milk.

Tofu

The best substitute I would recommend for Tofu is seitan, which is made from wheat gluten, thus making it an excellent substitute for meat. While the texture is dissimilar to tofu, it can be used as meat in chilis and soups as it is also high in protein level. Remember that some seitan may be soy-flavored.

In case you are finding it challenging to get some healthy seitan with no soy, you can make your own at home from wheat flour. When shopping, ensure that you carefully read the labels so you may buy the right substitute you need.

Sour Cream

I know Tofutti's Sour Supreme as the main dairy-free sour cream substitute. It is a vegan sour cream that has a strong tart flavor. It is also very thick, thus requires better planning before using it, especially in baking. To thin it, you may use some mild-tasting milk option before you combine into the batter.

Bread Crumbs

There are several bread crumb alternatives in the market. These include the stale bread, which fits the needs of your allergy. There is also the Pesach crumbs that are based on starch. They are made by Paskesz and can be found mostly during Passover.

Tortilla crumbs, which are also wheat-free, are also accessible in some supermarkets. In some recipes, you can also use cornmeal conversely with breadcrumbs. This is a safe alternative for anybody with no corn intolerance or allergy. These gluten-free and wheat-free bread crumbs can be found in brands like Aleia's gluten-free panko crumbs and Ian's gluten-free panko bread crumbs.

Pasta

There are many dried pasta in the market for those avoiding eggs. They are made from water and semolina. Fettucine and spaghetti, which are flat kinds of pasta, are most likely egg-free. Ensure that you inquire of the fresh pasta at restaurants. This is because pasta that has been made from scratch is most likely to have eggs.

There are also bean pasta, rice pasta, grain-based pasta, as well as pasta made from corn and a blend of corn and quinoa. These kinds of pasta are gluten-free and wheat-free, with rice pasta being the most common of them all. Compared to the usual pasta, these allergen-friendly substitutes are a bit different in taste and texture. For this reason, the option you take fully depends on your dietary needs and preference. Brands making these pasta substitutes are Ancient Harvest, Bionaturae, Tinkyada, Glutino, and Lundberg.

Tree Nuts

When taking a snack, you can use roasted sunflower seeds or pumpkin seeds, which are very healthy. They are crunchy, salty, and better options for those allergic to tree nut. You can use them shelled as substitutes to pine nuts when making pestos. In some recipes, you can also use these shelled pumpkin seeds as substitutes for almonds. Ensure that you review the details on the package to make sure that the product does not hold a cross-contamination risk from nuts, which may also be manufactured from the same place.

Cereal

These allergen-friendly cereals are beginning to grow more accessible at mainstream groceries. Some of these allergen-free cereals are Enjoy Life cereals, Zoe's (nut-free), Perky's, and Erewhon. Another alternative would be to use single-grain hot cereals, warm rice cereal, or pure oatmeal for breakfast.

Flour

To substitute flour with a wheat allergen-free alternative may need more than a specific kind of flour. This is because there is no simple alternative for the kinds of flour available.

Luckily, various companies produce baking mixes that are gluten-free and can work as direct wheat flour replacements. Brands with these kinds of replacement are like Bob's Red

Mill, Pamela's, and King Arthur, which all provide gluten-free baking mixes.

Cake Mix

During special occasions, you can try to find allergy-friendly producers with replacements for this product. One of the most generally accessible kind is from Cherrybrook Kitchen. It is fit for a lot of allergy demands, including tree nuts, dairy, peanuts, gluten, and eggs. You can find gluten-free mixes and dedicated wheat from Whole Foods and Pamela's. However, these are free of multi allergens.

Bread

There is a wide variety of ready-made healthy bread available in mainstream supermarkets for those avoiding gluten or wheat. In Whole Foods, a gluten-free bakery, you will find baked goods. Ener-G, Kinnikinnick Foods, and Glutino are also other stores where you can get gluten and wheat-free bread. They are generally the best toasted types of bread. You will mostly find the gluten-free bread at the freezer section in most supermarkets.

There is also egg-free bread, which is also somewhat common. However, check the labels when purchasing them. Orgran produces gluten-free, yeast-free, egg-free, whereas

Ener-G markets yeast-free and egg-free bread fermented with rice.

Peanut Butter

Sunbutter, soy butter, and pumpkin seed butter are the closest substitute to peanut butter available in supermarkets. If you are okay with tree nuts, you can use the tree nut butter, unless you are allergic to peanuts. When it comes to sandwiches, you can incorporate some inventive options to peanut butter together with ingredients that have a similar taste to peanut butter.

Trail Mix

There are a lot of options when it comes to trail mix. However, the main allergens that can hardly be avoided are options are on the market, but the major allergens that are difficult to avoid here are tree nuts and peanuts. Incase of sulfite and dried fruit mixes, you can make your own mix from a simple recipe.

Canned Tomatoes

It is obvious that you cannot find a tomato-free replacement for canned tomatoes. However, a lot of canned tomatoes are processed with corn. The good thing is, it is possible to make your own peeled tomatoes that are free from corn hassle-free.

To do this, slice an "X" at the top and bottom of a ripened tomato and immerse it for about five minutes in boiling water. Take it out of the hot water and let it cool until it can be handled easily. When ready, you should be able to easily peel off the tomato skin. This is the time that you also remove the seeds. Use immediately after you make it and store the rest for about a week in the fridge in a covered container.

Beer

Fortunately, beers that are free of gluten and wheat are gradually becoming more publicly available in the market. Anheuser-Busch's Redbridge brand is the most readily-available kind in the whole nation.

For anyone allergic to corn, it is important to note that most beers available in the market are made from corn. But, a lot of beers from German origin are not. When the word "Reinheitsgebot" is used on a German beer, that means that the booze is produced from water, yeast, hops, and barley only. It is, however, sensible to confirm this from the producer before you drink it.

Conclusion

As you can now see, it is very easy to make your own restaurant kinds of food and save yourself some money. These dishes can be made healthier, and you can make many of them to share with friends.

You can make my favorite banana pancakes for breakfast, a bowl of burritos for lunch, some bourbon chicken with some coleslaw side dish for dinner, or even some blonde brownies for dinner. All these you can make in the comfort of your home.

Ensure that you observe health measures with some of the healthy substitutes that I have also suggested in the book.

I hope you get to try these yummy delicacies and get a feel of the palatal heaven I am talking about.

If this book has helped or inspired you in any way, would you please consider leaving me a review? I would appreciate it.